Wisdom & Vision

Wisdom & Vision

70 Inspiring Poems
on How to Live A Meaningful Life

Alex K. Warren

authorHOUSE®

AuthorHouse™ LLC
1663 Liberty Drive
Bloomington, IN 47403
www.authorhouse.com
Phone: 1-800-839-8640

Published by AuthorHouse   08/19/2013

ISBN: 978-1-4817-7479-6 (sc)
ISBN: 978-1-4817-7480-2 (e)

Library of Congress Control Number: 2013912517

Any people depicted in stock imagery provided by Thinkstock are models, and such images are being used for illustrative purposes only.
Certain stock imagery © Thinkstock.

This book is printed on acid-free paper.

Because of the dynamic nature of the Internet, any web addresses or links contained in this book may have changed since publication and may no longer be valid. The views expressed in this work are solely those of the author and do not necessarily reflect the views of the publisher, and the publisher hereby disclaims any responsibility for them.

Contents

Introduction

I want to start off by saying I do not have life figured out. Not by a long shot. However, through my own life experiences I was able to pick up some wisdom; emphasis on the word "some". The reason I decided to write this book was to inspire others. I only hope that some of my own life experiences, shown throughout this book, exemplifies to anyone who reads it that everyone has purpose. Everyone has the right to a happy and meaningful life. My poetry however is not like most poetry, or so I've been told. Does that mean it's the best? No, not even close.

I simply envisioned poetry in a different way; a way in which rhyme, realistic outlooks, and optimistic thoughts could be blended together. It comes out of a personal belief of mine. People need to see life from a different angle in order to view life completely for what it truly is. At times it is an opportunity to make up for past mistakes. In life we all will have the opportunity to be the next big thing. But these are simply my thoughts.

These poems are meant to encourage you to take a deeper look at yourself, your experiences, and your best qualities. They are meant for you to understand three things: Yourself, Life, and God. If you don't believe in God, then it's simply two things. Or maybe this will help you to see God? Who knows?

Regardless, this is not meant to be read as a religious testimony. I hope it will encourage you to think of a solution to different problems you may be facing rather than on all of your problems. There is no right or wrong way to interpret these writings so if you do not comprehend some of them in the way you feel you should, do not be discouraged. I guarantee there will be at least one in which you will connect with deeply, and that one was meant for you. All I ask is for you to sit back, relax, and enjoy.

Insight: College Days

I remember my freshmen year in college. It was at a small community school, in a very small city. It was the end of the quarter and I was on my way home to see what grades I received in my classes. After going online and checking my grades I realized that I had failed three classes, and got "C's" in the others. It was at that moment that I thought to myself, "Am I really smart enough for school? Is school really worth the trouble?" I remember talking to my parents and my brother, telling them I was disappointed in the grades. Their responses were pretty interesting, only because I remember my high school days. Whenever I got a bad grade my parents would say things like "you can do better" or "try harder next time" but, college was different. College was my time to realize that I am a man, no longer a kid. In a way, I'm no longer living everyday just to abide by the rules.

No longer am I getting up to do the same thing every day. After high school it's all about the choices I to make. So when I told my parents about this, they said, "You know what, it happens. You'll do better next time." When I told my brother he kind of just laughed and said, "I've been there. It sucks but you keep going and, you do better."

When the next quarter came around I had taken three classes instead of five. I didn't really work that much harder, but there was a difference. At the end of the quarter I found out I had two A's and a B. It was a complete turnaround from my first quarter, even though I had taken harder classes this time. It was then that I realized that life isn't about being smart enough, being strong enough, being fast enough, or even being first.

Life is about the choices that you make. Even in the hardest times. I remember after I had recieved those grades after the first quarter I wanted to dropout. I didn't want to go back or even try again. But I realized I had a choice to make. I could either give up, call it a day; or, I could try again.

It came to the point where it was my last quarter of my freshmen year in college. I had to take at least five classes in order to transfer to the college that I wanted to go to. I couldn't get anything less than a B+. Those five classes included Psychology (with the head psychologist in the major), an advanced math class (which was ridiculously hard and pointless), a science course, a Spanish course, and a Russian course. Even to this day I'm still not sure why I had to take the last one.

I ended up taking those classes. The lowest grade I got was a B+. I knew for a fact I wasn't the brightest kid. Not dumb, just not top of the class. But regardless of that, I knew that in life, no matter how hard things may have seemed, I always had a choice.

CHAPTER 1

Chapter 1: Happiness

Throughout life people seek one thing; happiness. They may not know it, but it's a common goal across the world. When you realize happiness is the key goal for success, you'll begin to make the right changes in your life. Throughout my life I've found happiness by aligning my feelings with what I want to happen. For instance, if I wanted to work out and get in shape I would get myself to "feel" like working out and getting in shape. The same goes for happiness. You have to find out what brings it to you. It doesn't hurt to seek advice. If you do that and keep a faithful attitude, you will cause things to change.

Possessions and achievements don't bring you real happiness, and it's not an easy thing to find. It takes deep thought and a lot of soul searching in order to find out what truly makes you happy. Don't get me wrong, there's nothing wrong with having possessions. We all have them and we all enjoy them, but they will never fill the hole we all have. First thing you need to do is to ask yourself, "Where is my happiness?" and when found, "How do I maintain it?" These next writings offer some suggestions on how to find real happiness.

Where's Your Happiness?

Where's your happiness? Has it been lost at the
cost for possessions or an obsession with material
objects? Or, is it simply infused when you choose
to find a new person in your life? No matter what, it
cuts deep into our mind to see how fine the amount
is of our joy. Seeming coy, we do not have nearly
enough. The fluff in our life gives strife an open gate
to relate with our emotions. The commotion leaves
us troubled, or doubled in our sadness. But this is
madness. Why not be happy? No fool does rule with
a satirically, depressive attitude. We must own it
as our own responsibility to see what truly makes
happiness for us all. For we fall every day yet we
say we're "alright", when we should be better than
just that. The stack of obstacles against us requires
trust in our attitude. Though the brute of monsters
we battle try to rattle our thinking, optimism gives
us hope. Not to just cope, but to thrive and strive for
better than normal lives in which we want. So to be
blunt, ask yourself this question; for the neglection of
doing so will grow a disastrous existence. Through all
persistence is an ending worth spending your energy
on. Though not gone in gladness, just ask this; where
is your happiness?

Take Me Back to Those Days

Take me back to the days when time was slow.
Slow enough to where sand and simple plans were
equal to fun. Fun being what one could do for others
without the setting of the Sun at the end of the day.
Days, in which we confided and guided those, not
only asking but basking in the need for help. Help
in which was never given, yet forgiven, for sins live
within and are rinsed out. Out of mind and be it so
kind not to remind us of what we did. Did we really
mean to do it though? Or was our mind too slow
to know the gravity of which our actions had taken
effect? Regardless, some think it marvelous what we
can make it through. Through the storms and thick
weather, we stick together; but who do you stick to?
The brother man or the other man, or maybe just
the mother with a plan for her own son's life. Life
without the pain yet with the gain of success; yes,
that's the life she strived for in us. Us, and all those
who fuss about being lost and not knowing what's
what. Yeah, take me back to those days, not with
maids and chefs, but simple times when Geoff and
Will took on our TV. My bad I meant Geoffrey, but
don't you see what I mean? Those were the times
that refined my youth. Not to conclude but interlude
the struggles of the hustle in life. Yeah, those days
in which a simple switch could turn a sad May into
happy days. Where no fear was clear, but friends

stayed near, just to be sincere and show that they meant something. Well, not just something, but smoothly showed that we could be bold; we could be the light to this world. Yeah, I'm just saying, with no delays; simply take me back to those days.

A Wider Gaze

There's always more to see in life. Some distant treasures never measure up to the simple pleasures you can enjoy every day. It seems that there is a sequence of pretense happiness, waiting for us all to experience. Though they are here, they never seem near enough to be found. Sometimes it's like a maze or trying to pass through each phase of a stage, or a staggering amount of courses. We employ our best efforts to sever our past sadness. Is it madness to say there are better days ahead? I don't think so. It's good to have a challenge so we don't binge and waste our happiest days. Each second there is a special moment to witness. Our fitness relies on our own compromise that gives us a chance to see a wider range in our own lives. True happiness only comes when one is ready to see it. If you only see failure and think of things not so pure, the ringing in your head will be no comfort to your bed of peace. Basically, you have to see it before it can happen. Your imagination leads to the creation of reality. If your outlook is dim then within the nature of your thought will sooner or later come out. If you can imagine better days there will be nothing that can phase you. You have to be proactive. Only then will you see, the true beauty, of this life.

A Summer Breeze

A new summer breeze is starting to ease my mind. I find the peace pretty relaxing. No acting in the part, the visual art of nature is entrancing. Some camping may be in order, to border between the lines of happiness, and hope. To cope through this heat is a very easy feat, indeed. Proceed with your sunbathing. It's making the walk to go talk to a neighbor that truly does favor this season. No other reason but that does relax my soul. Goals are now being made. Stayed in the hour I devour this time with activities. Proclivity isn't the option, but auctions are attended for those who are intended to buy. I sigh when others stress at this time . . . . I'm sorry. I'm simply stating what I see with no truly held beliefs. But what I'm trying to say is that every day you should take time out to just enjoy the view. Soothe your heart with a start of positive thinking by bringing the outside in. Begin with a message, that sound investments will arise. Don't agonize over what happened yesterday. Pay this day a compliment. No need to repent, because what God sent is a second chance. Take your stance in the matter by reducing the clatter and noise. Realize those lies no longer affect you. Hold on to the truth of the day. After a winter's tease, we have alas found this new, summer breeze.

Insight: Why not?

Everyday life throws something new at us. Maybe you wake up to find you've overslept. Maybe you got off work, just in time to find someone has smashed your car window. Or maybe, your day just didn't go as planned. Don't worry; at least one of these events has happened to all of us. So what do we do? Do we look around to find a rock and smash someone else's car? I hope not.

A bad circumstance is just that; circumstantial. They happen once but they will not last. We often choose to let these circumstances ruin our day. We think "if this would've happened my day would've been perfect". Few realize that happiness rarely comes from perfect days. Happiness is deeper than that. It's a point of view. It's the right perspective.

Its patience, something we all seem to lack. But being truly happy is a choice. Not a dependency on what does or doesn't happen throughout the day. In essence, everyday could be a good day. And good days produce success, or at least the ability to achieve one's goals. So why not choose to be happy?

CHAPTER 2

Chapter 2: Love

What is poetry without love? It's nothing short of a miracle to be able to fall in love with someone. What if I told you romance was also a necessary key to having true success and happiness? As human beings we all want to be loved for who we are; flaws and all. We strive for that and to get someone to love us takes a huge amount of effort. Unfortunately it can be painful; at least until you find the perfect fit. Many times it will take envisioning your future in order to make things come to pass. Whether it is envisioning a future company, or seeing yourself as a NBA player.

Same goes also go for love. Yes, even we as men have to do it. Not everyone is a sappy romantic, and I have to admit, I'm far from it myself. Yet, I know how important it is to find love. Love inspires us to achieve more. When we know we are loved it does something to us. It builds up our strength and gives us an overcoming mindset. The people we love boost our self-esteem and brings us confidence. It can also change a person. Love at its very basic level can bring great results. The following writings will express the depths of love's effects and demonstrates why it is so important.

The Principle of Love

Love is something else, isn't it? It twists us up, just
enough, to make us feel invincible. The principle of it
is . . . .

Well, no one really knows. Yes, we take some blows
to find it, but once it's legit it does fit us perfectly
with the person we fell for. They neither bore nor
excite us, but instead they reunite us with our soul.
We are forever filled, in a bag zipped and sealed with
two hearts. It's the jump start to our morning. We
are warning the day that dismay will no longer affect
us. Simply, because our soul mate won't let it. They
bring out the best for any test life does throw our way.
They sway our trust, just enough to make it rough,
or almost nearly impossible, for any outside thing
to hurt us. Our souls are intertwining and aligning
the destinies of one combined spirit. They clear it
all for us to see. Not just to believe but to conceive
of the idea in which it truly does take two to make
one. Fun is now our new option. At the drop of a pin
they begin to descend to our level and push our own
pedals into gear. They take fear to be sincere, showing
us that with them, there is nothing to be afraid of.
Like a dove we fly high to supernatural skies, only
love has allowed us to reach. With no breach in the
contract, we contact a sensual feeling of happiness.
We're blessed in this Heaven where we let in, or out,

how we do feel. With appeal, they will reel out what you have been hiding so long; humming softly with a song, they whisper how it's alright. No fight does conclude, instead, the mood of the moment does bring you closer. You look over in their eyes and size up the beauty of the universe, in one simple being. So seeing how this love does bring, a sting of great things; love really is, something else.

I Know You

I know you. Well I mean, I've never really met
you before, but I do know you. A beautiful soul
with plenty of goals and ambition. Never asking
permission, but proving to all religions that there
is a God. It may seem odd; beauty like yours is an
angelic nod from above. Your eyes show love like
the flutter of a dove in flight. My God, I've never
seen such a sight in my life. All strife together has
left me, only to believe what I truly can now see. The
way you walk with grace, putting forth the race, or
racing should I say, of my heart. I never knew art,
but a smart man once told me, "be bold to seek what
the soul needs," and that is you. The true you, and
battles you have went through, take nothing back.
They give wonder, not slack, to what's wrapped in
your ostentatious, yet gracious smile. The way you
stride and glide like there's no one on either side of
you. This is new, I mean really new, how there is
no shrewdness or rudeness throughout your body.
With no luck would I have you, but grace and mercy
would have to grasp you, for me. My, would I be
pleased to fulfill your every need, since greed has no
part in any of your anatomy. I'd grab the moon and
leave soon to show it how your beauty compares to
no one. Only the rising of the Sun could have won,
yet, only compared to the moon; surely, it'd fair
poorly compared to you. The way you fit together

brings light to my stormy weather, filled with rain and clouds. No doubt should I pout if you are not mine. I'd sing every record or turn to a beggar, just to show me how to gain your trust. Its cause trust is a must, in which without it would result in the greatest lust for deceit. With deceit being cheap it would reap me no benefit. It would have to be real. Real to the point where I feel all my joints rebuild; where a tingle down my spine, would incline me, to be the very best thing in the world, simply to deserve you. So yes its true, I do know you. Although I've never met you before, you are my perfect metaphor for who I wish to meet. So with this, I do greet you with bliss in saying; I know you.

Winning the Quarrel

Through love and strength I've come to see.

There is no quarrel that has no seed.

They sometimes come from daily things.

Like work, driving, or what life brings.

Regardless, something's bound to stir.

But always does it start with her.

Her emotions just take control.

It won't make sense, and guys, we stall.

We wait to see what she says next.

And hope her words will soon make sense.

And yet, they don't; what do we do?

Should we barge in and end this feud?

Hmmm . . .

Probably not, we all know why.

We know one word can end our lives.

Yet in her way, she will not stop.

If we do run, she'll throw the pot.

Now fast or not, no man can say.

He's ever that quick to dodge away.

For we've all tried with same results.

We wake to a nurse who's waving salt.

So now we're stuck, she's adding on.

Her arguments being far from done.

Our choices now, are down to two.

We could give up and say we're through.

Let's all be honest, we just want food.

And arguing won't set the mood.

We could just add, some gas to fire.

But in the end we'll both be tired.

The smart move is, to just give up.

For then there's food, and also luck.

So really guys, we know it must end.

We get what we want, along with the win.

Just know this one fact, that does deal with quarrels.

That no one can win if you don't have a girl.

Just know that each day there's a message that's sent.

Though one quarrel does end, another begins.

Know that if you choose, to go and fight back.

You'll die of starvation and have to get packed.

For all girls are crazy; though, they seem so still.

We must choose to love them if we want our fill.

This way they might cook, and soon set the mood.

So pleasure does come, along with your food.

Finding My Way

I'm still finding my way in this world. No hurdle can stop me, but plots do drop me in different situations. There's a sensation of problems and to solve them proves to be a challenge. The puzzle continually gains more pieces. Yet it never ceases to amaze or haze the fact that it won't last long. My throng in life casts a broader shadow. Though the gallows are wet, you can bet on the case that I will win. It begins with a plan. What do I understand to be the question? Could it be the reflection of an emotional meaning? As a human being, it is possible; although, very unlikely. By signing my thoughts, I brought upon my own deeper search to find my inner self. What newfound stealth has my subconscious brought upon me? This is interesting, but tiring to think on. No pawn takes the king, with the queen still depending on the king to protect the throne. But wait . . . that's it! I have no one yet to call my queen. It seems this does deem my problem solvable; although, gullible is the person seeking real love. Only above is it given, but here it must be earned. We learn how to trust and rid lust from our friendship. No penmanship should draw in the girl. With a whirl of luck, I would pluck her out of the crowd. Yet loud is the sound of a resounding echo from beings of distraction. My reaction must be consistent with my need. The seed must be planted and I, invested, for my own sake. Mistakes happen;

but, that's okay. What gives way will make it well worth it. It seems fit to say this because bliss is amazing when shared with the one you love. Another day I guess, I will see this come true. But through the time being, I'll be patient in seeing this come to pass. Outlasting a true pearl, I will then, truly, find my way in this world.

A Different Breed

You're clearly a different breed. I proceed to want
to see you. True are your words that seem to concur
with beauty. Truly you came from afar. No star shines
brighter and your mind does desire the best. I detest
the fact that I have reacted in such a shyish way.
Some say you're angelic, when even ancient relics
couldn't describe your godly features. You're the
teacher, in your ways, which leaves me in dismay
when you talk. Walk as you may, I guarantee that
each day is better with you in it. I don't get how I'm
just now meeting you. Soothed is the soul that fails
every goal, yet still manages to see your smile. Files
are made when you are displayed to the public. "She's
fake" most girls say, but they're envious in ways that
would disgust nature itself. It's amazing. I'm gazing
at your eyes only to fail to devise a proper intro.
As fate goes, I feel bold enough to make a move.
Smooth are my thoughts though a knot is forming in
my chest. It's best to see that suddenly, you said hi.
To my surprise this was all just the beginning. I think
that's when I knew, you were guaranteed to truly be, a
different breed.

CHAPTER 3

Chapter 3: Encouragement

It's hard to make it through life when it throws you a curveball for no reason. It's even harder when you don't have any encouragement. Encouragement is a strong factor when it comes to achieving anything. It's our motivation, our inspiration, and our reason for becoming better. Many times encouragement comes from parents and friends. They help you to stay focused and never give up. However, it isn't always easy to find encouraging people. Perhaps your parents were just the opposite. There's only one thing you can do about that; forget and ignore them. It's important that you ignore those who try to bring you down.

Ignoring your haters, like finding happiness, is not easy. You have to make an honest effort to find people who are encouraging. This counteracts the effects of any negativity. Once you realize your own potential, your perspective on life changes. It's always necessary to have an inner circle filled with encouraging people. These same people in your inner circle will help you find success. The following writings will encourage you to not only be successful, but will also encourage you to be a better you.

You're Greater Than You Think

You are greater than you think. I know it's a hard
thing to grasp, but that's not the task at hand. God
has a great plan for you to go and seek truth in
your own way. It's not every day that this happens.
To even tap in to your talents is a feat many retreat
from, but you don't. You won't give into your past
difficulties that reappear through new trials. But
all the while know this; you can get past them all.
You won't fall to society's touch of not having
much, but instead you'll lead the group that needs
to see you succeed. You have a gift. One that will
shift this nation from all wrongful installations,
in which many experience. Through this period
there will be struggles, but it will be well worth
the trouble when you reach the outcome. You are
not dumb but bright to light this ambitious torch
that scorches all failure. You are the carrier of
something innately inside that will guide you to
the finish line. So even if we don't speak again I
know that within you lies something great. In this
state you gain such a grateful bunch of trust; not
with all others, but simply with yourself. You'll
provide your own wealth and cures to things not
pure in life. You'll thrive in helping everyone to
see the true Son of God which others may say is
odd but pay them no attention. For the dimension
you are about to enter into will bring mysteries of

wonder among you and a great truth will be yours to hand out. So without a doubt get ready to count your coming blessings. Cause truly, you are greater than you think.

This Is True

This is true. My talents are such that they are greater than much of what I expected. Reflected upon the promise of lost thoughts being gone; I do submit to the awe of what's enthralled in my spirit. Do you hear it? Through rescue and search I've never been so perched on just one idea. See you didn't even think I'd be on the brink of such a discovery. Simply it's a tree for thought, but the food did rot without the root to suck up the filled cup of true nutrients. I do repent for the wrong I've done but hear the gospels of the songs not sung, through which my spirit does sing. Bring me your worry and I'll help you to burry your past so it does not outlast your successful premonition. With the ignition of great thought, you ought to know the more is the better, as long as you never do it simply to be the greatest. Instead be the latest to see that your spirit is key to finding and being who you truly are. We are all far from seeing ourselves as truly talented beings with the capacity to change the world. Through a curling range of different gains our gifts do shift the worst perspective beliefs. Don't retrieve from this thought. For what's brought from it is understanding. The demanding accounts for not being renounced as just another person. What yearns will guide you to mystic truths that will soothe your soul. The goal is never too much for such a being as yourself. You are filled with inner wealth and stealth from the harmful lies. Deprive your mind of thoughts of failure. It's not regular for you to be average, but rather the cabbage giving life to the soulless rabbit that strives for peace. Just ease your mind into this state to help relate your spirit in this rightful place. Space between the opinionated facts will not distract you from your purpose. Not to be shrewd or rude but your meaning in life is prudent to making it better for us all. Don't fall from the proof because this, my friend, will bring aloof a greater you. So yes, all-in-all I hope to install in you, that simply, this is true.

The Winning Soul

Make some noise for Life's return,

And meet it in the street.

For Life's got much to celebrate,

Once beating all Defeat.

It ran the race, a marathon,

And stumbled halfway through.

No water handed toward its way,

Yet strength still remained true.

Through most the race it had to fight,

It had no inner peace.

It tried and tried to fight and hide,

But nothing came with ease.

It came to see just one true thing,

That kept it going on.

A promise given for glory,

To show that it had won.

But dizzy and still yet confused,

Life didn't understand.

The race itself was still at work,

And losing was the plan.

But through surprise and no demise,

The promise was kept still.

For Life believed this promise now,

The race became a thrill.

Defeat was sprinting on its way,

And looked right back at Life.

It laughed and ran all through the night,

But Life took on no strife.

Life took some pride and jogged with stride,

To keep its rightful pace.

And through the day just hummed a song,

To just enjoy the race.

The finish line was just in sight,

About 300 feet.

Life looked around and broke a sweat,

To see or find Defeat.

And there it was, laid on the ground,

No air to it insight.

With this now known Life took a breath,

And gave it all its might.

Life crossed the line to find it won,

The race now being done.

With great applause they cheered Life on,

To thank Life for its run.

With this now known to all around,

All people can now see.

That Hope gave Life the promise that,

Would give us victory.

So when you think you've faced Defeat,

Know that you still can win.

For Life and Hope have promised it,

But know it starts within.

And soon enough you'll finish too,

With nothing but a smile.

For this is how we're meant to live,

Not losing all the while.

So take a breath and jog this race,

Enjoy it and go slow.

For Life and Hope give victory,

We have The Winning Soul.

Dreams Come True

It's hard to believe that our dreams can come true.
Young in our youth the truth on the matter was
lost. The cost to make something happen is always
more than we expected. Yet, we dare not neglect our
dreams. We seem to actually, in our best attempts,
keep them alive. We strive for the reincarnation when
they die, and deny the fact that they may never come
back. Though, distract that from being the end. We
tend to see others accomplish their dreams, so why
not accomplish our own? Is it sown somewhere that
our life of despair is permanent? No way! Each day
gives birth to making our dreams happen. We tap in
to our talents and valiantly we work harder than we
thought we could. We stood at the bottom to then
cause some to notice our dreams really are, existent.
Persistently we stay on track to the fact that one day it
will happen; our dreams will be a realization of things
that can be achieved. No thieves can take this, just
believe to make bliss in realizing, that your dreams
can, come true.

New Beginnings

Few can feel the pain I've felt,

From loss and great defeat.

But few can also dust it off,

And get back on their feet.

You see each year I come to find,

Mistakes both here and there.

Regardless of the work I've done,

I fall so very near.

It's when perfection's at my grasp,

That suddenly it leaves.

And like a moth drawn to the light,

I dare not let it flee.

One day it came unto a point,

Where I just felt so lost.

When suddenly my friends appeared,

Yet they all seemed in awe.

They asked, "How could you feel so down?"

No man can be perfect.

This year was great I reached new heights,

But never did reflect.

Realizing this, I then stood up,

Now that I knew the truth.

I might have grasped no perfect thing,

Yet, perfection lives in you.

It keeps you strong when you feel weak,

And lifts your head up high.

It keeps your feet on solid ground,

When others try to fly.

It motivates the near hopeless,

To help them through mistakes.

It shows them past all their failure,

For it's a path few take.

So next time when you're feeling down,

Rise up and know one thing.

If you fell not you'd never move,

And make new beginnings.

Daily Purpose

What's the purpose for today? Is it to display what
delays have held us up in life? No, I don't think so.
Maybe it's to show what's reality when all actuality
ceases to exist. We assist each other in the process.
We find common sense through wisdom and kid
none with a childish like dream. We scheme to
the top to stop any unbelievers. We're achievers
basically, in our own right. We fight to give value
through how you should really live. Not to give
but to receive what others believe to be a mistake.
Don't take what's not yours though. Grow in the
knowledge that college isn't the only place to get
an education. Our relation in this life is that we all
deal with strife, and eventually, we overcome it. Not
to be fit and show off, but to sit and read soft, or
softly, to our following generations. The sensation
that's felt will be dealt to all those who are doing
the dealing. Reaching the ceilings and farther don't
seem to bother the ambitious man. He plans for the
rain when his simple domains have no control. He
trolls for the honest to bring promise to what would
otherwise be meaningless living. He's giving hope.
"Nope" is the answer for those who have cancer
with no tumor. Otherwise known as a rumor they
humor the idea of never getting better. Whether
this was you, it doesn't have to be true for long. Go
along with this theory and really you'll see it should

be a law. Sit in awe at what crawled to the surface.
Emerging is the kind but very fine statements. It
seems blatant to comment but nonsense could hide
its tracks. It's just a fact. We must act now to show
how we can achieve any dream. This would only
truly seem, to be the purpose for today.

Failure and Success

Failure seems to be a must. In everything I've done I've been the one to fail first. I'd get the F on the test when the rest of the class did their best. I never understood why. I would try and study or find a group of buddies to help me out. Still, I would fail. It wasn't till later on when I spawned my way into college that something became noticeable. I did better with failure. Not to say I continued in low grades, but my highest spade came after failure. My perseverance gave me some clearance in class. I didn't amass straight A's, but I did get close. The harder I tried, the more unified my thoughts became. It could've been physics or even statistics, but I would do well in the end. It's all because I wouldn't, or maybe I couldn't let failure have the last say. Each day I'd put aside my pride and guide my way to making A's, even when I didn't understand. I demanded better, whether I deserved it or not. Only failure opened my eyes to learn the disguise of what it was truly hiding. Success, through perseverance. Never hiding in mind, I'd find how to overcome the most difficult test. It's a pest to do this but through it I came out even better. So never get down when you have found out you did badly. Understand that you must withstand failure in order to demand success.

Don't Stop Now

Please, don't stop now. The cloud of your judgment
is causing resentment to your gift. The talent in
which brings a glitch to life's lost system. No
person is dumb but only forgets to thumb down and
hone in on their gift. They thrift and lift their heads
higher for wrongful desires. Let's say for things,
like money, gambling or pleas of guilty attitudes.
Not to be rude but defuse your egotistical thoughts.
Never sought for their talent some people can't
grasp it in time. They rewind on back to the times
of lack and premonition. The fission of such gets
them only as much as they can see. Yet believe
me, the eye cannot see everything. Distinctions of
success press the subconscious mind. It is destined
to find, in time, the greatest feats in life. Not quite
the delight most of us do think of, for love is a drug
in which no one above can concede of as being
wrong; yet, this is not the only thing the mind
desires. Happiness is a must through which goes on
to bust any level of sadness. But isn't that the test?
Going through pain, up against the grain of life to
come out as a winner? Yet we're only beginners
when it comes to this. Bliss and mercy give our
talents the courtesy to own everything a person
could need. Whether you're good at just biking,
or maybe it's your writing that seems to touch the
world in a special way. So stop today with your

pith of childish thinking. Continue on to be gone from this misery. This way the whole world can see how it's not lost but soon found; simply, because you didn't stop now.

Make a Mistake

What does it mean to make a mistake? Does it take
away the chance in a day to do right? I'd hope not.
We try to learn and then discern which choice is best.
But then we have the little pest of being wrong. I
believe in a song it said something along those lines.
Only losers are beggars who chose on whether they
would learn, or simply keep on for a penny. Simply
said, how are we led to deal with our bad choices?
We hear the voices and notice the noises of regret.
How will they be silenced? Basic science, known
as common sense, shows recompense or repentance
is best. Admit you're wrong and go along believing
for better. Your feelings may only seem to go in the
opposite direction. That is okay. Every day they do
sway, not knowing what is what. But, they are not in
charge. You are. You have the last say and can pray
on whatever you would like. You can fight with your
might, or huddle over in the corner. Those voices
are choices of which you can listen to, or get rid of.
Regardless, above is a being, seeing what choices you
make. For your sake, make the choice that is pleasing
to him. Grim are the thoughts of what ought to be
right, and turn out wrong. All you can do is prove that
you have purpose. The circus in life comes to bring
strife to those who are not focused. It's bogus when
people say you cannot make it. See fit to prove them
wrong so no throng can pick you out to be the loser.

Never defer to prefer the idea that you can't make mistakes. It may take a lot to bounce back, but the slack you avoid is never more annoyed when it sees your results are success. Mistakes make the best test to prove to the rest that you indeed, will be blessed in the end. I only recommend that you tend to this knowledge. You never know that it all could just take one mistake, to start the beginning of a very bright future.

Forget About the Past

Forget about the past. It means nothing but something
to cause pain. We gain no satisfaction from the
actions of our past. It will regress in its effect, yet
rejects our happiness because of our thoughts. Sought
out we must condemn them, being the thoughts, that
lend us no help. What's felt must go away in order for
us to stay on a successful path. For the wrath of such
should not be endured for it's absurd to live like that.
Being stacked against the odds the past does give nod
to more failure in your life. So basically; get over it.
Throwing fits will help no one only bringing down
the one Sun shining bright for your guide. People lied
when they said to look back but go ahead without
worries; for it is impossible. The probable cause of
worry comes from the line being blurry descending
from two choices; moving on or leaning on the past.
With nothing left to lose you might as well choose the
first option. From there you are caught in an eternal
destiny. One that few others can see due to their
wicked blindness, causing them to resent the truth. Do
not get caught in their booth. Instead, move ahead to
where you want to be. Success precedes those hungry
for needs of being better. Never tether on the line;
you are inclined to do so much more. What's in store
will never bore your cravings for righteousness. Be
blessed to know that you can show that at last, you
can now forget about your past.

You

Figuring out who you are is important. A lot are confused at who they want to choose to be. They see different actors and then try to factor in, if they can be that character or not. But we're not here to play roles. We were born to adorn, or be adored, by those who know us. So what makes you, you? It's all the things that seem to bring you stress. If you could accept who you are, as a person you'll go far and beyond what you could have ever comprehended to be possible. The way you walk and the speech in your talk, is you. The different actions and simple satisfactions you find, are you. The way you react to unexpected facts make you who you are. The way that you stumble where others would crumble to pieces, is who you are. Your distinctive mistakes and the time that it takes you to learn from them, clearly, makes up who you are. You should never be discouraged at the courage others show in different times. You may ask why. It's because only above it all, they fall where you succeed, and proceed to envy certain parts of your character. That is okay because in a way, we all have done this, but there is great promise in us all. If you accept who you are, no matter how far you are from being right, great things will come to take away any sorrow. So follow your weird actions that seem to bring satisfaction to yourself. This will always come to remain true, because there is no one in the world, like You.

Start Now

You should start now. From what I've learned you've earned so much in your life. Not simply to just please your pleasures, but to lay ground work for your future endeavors; this, in which will bring great success. Blessed is the mind so kind to have discipline. It's within that which we find our true calling; whether sprawling at opportunities or going to places just to see how far we can be pushed. No bush hides our true faults but no cult will be around you to condemn us. The fuss will be about the doubts everyone once had for you. Saying you couldn't make it through the pain yet now you have gained the world because of your own "just" thinking. Don't be satisfied with this though. You must grow in your youth to give proof that others can grow along with you. Like a tree in the forest no florist is around to groom what limbs have fallen off. Simply cough if you need help and what's dealt will be a helping hand for your situation. Destinations will always change but your pain and tolerance to rearrange the game will give you promising results. Your motto should be this; "I do not reminisce in my failure but I truly see that no one can shell my heart." At least in knowing this you'll get a head start to rightful thinking. The decision to be forgiven will show that ultimately, for success' sake; you should definitely start now.

Late Nights

I believe we all have late nights. Sitting awake, trying to mistake it for insomnia. But that's not it, is it? We think of our purpose and how we can surface to the top. You may be stuck in a dead job, or trying to sob your way through a lonely night. Regardless, you feel like right now, there's no way how the life you're living presently is enough. You want to help the sick, or try to flick away the pesky problems people face every day. It's not a depression, but the neglection of your inner soul, even when it's right. You are meant for much more. You were born to unite those who fight for a higher cause. You were born to inspire those who desire to become better people. You're not a sequel, but equal to the best beings in history. You're just seeking to find your purpose in life. I had those nights. Where success was all around, but no purpose was found for myself. My health was great and I could deeply relate to those around me. But my plea to see and do better, never let me sleep. I had many ways to deal with these days, though none worked. Working was all fun yet after all was said and done, I stayed awake. I worked every hour, till sour of the results, where I simply stayed up. Had some more work to jerk me out of keeping my eyes open, but the token to this game brought me shame, and sleep was still lost. It wasn't until I stood still, and thought about my purpose, that I found rest. It was the best remedy.

Things came together to weather better outcomes. So in case you faced this problem, it's solved when you find your true purpose in life. It will serve fit to stop your late nights, where might itself, is the one thing that cannot fix it. You must be bold and eventually told, that in this, we all began with late nights.

Start Your Business

Start your business. We've all heard the chorused
words of being an entrepreneur. To ensure we
have income we begin one of many things: a job, a
business, a robbery or a stimulus, and so on. But gone
is the idea to reveal our inner company. One with
no money but a thought, of what's bought and sold
on a daily basis. It's the faceless owners who make
the most money. Sounds funny doesn't it? But it's
truthfully so, that to grow our own business we must
look within. What dims our interests and what sparks
our sinless behavior? What do we love above all other
things? See, it's not gadgets that factor into making
millions. Sometimes a billion things do not ring up
the checks we want. But what makes you happy will
gladly bring you the income you wish to have. During
this path you will find that your mind is much deeper
and neater than you could've ever imagined. So a
billionaire knows it's fair to seek inside what will
guide him to his next idea. What entrances his soul
does give bold recollection of what will come next.
No pretext is given but living in our inner dwellings
through the melting pot of ideas; it comes together. So
just remember, your sadness turns to gladness when
your interest finally helps you, to start a business.

Something in Every Day

There's something in everyday. You could be at
the bus-stop or be at a chill spot and still notice
something new. Maybe a person stops to talk while
you walk down the street. Making small chat or
giving stats on the basketball game from last night.
Either way everyday seems to bring something
nice and enjoyable like that. It's like a pat on the
back from life itself, to wish you good health on the
many journeys you have planned. You can't demand
these nice things to happen though. They go with
how you sow your time. If you're willing to give a
thrilling amount of money to the homeless, you'll be
rewarded. But maybe this doesn't mean much to you.
Maybe a person saying "hi" or watching a person
"try" to help out the elderly doesn't' give you joy.
If so, I feel sorry for you. The true moments of life
happen in this. Noticing the small things could bring
a level of understanding to you that you couldn't have
possibly found out any other way. You have to play
with this idea to make it real. Feel the meal that each
day is trying to give you. Be fed by what has led your
heart to this very place. Sometimes its nothing which
brings something you've always needed. Regardless,
its hard when you choose and refuse to lose sight, that
there is something in everyday.

A Better Future

My choice for the future is better. No weather of
the sorts, will report me of doing differently. What I
see will be key to being, what I'm retrieving to be.
Simply put, my desires will be higher; it's the flyer
of the buyer who owns this kite. Not short of any
might, I will fight; and I will succeed. Proceeding
in this glory, my story, will be great. It relates to the
message of my life. My strife will not last, because
my past will not matter. I scatter the thoughts of
defeat. Like the feet that are washed, I have squashed
all negative thinking. Seeking a journey that hurts me,
will no longer exist. In this tense no briefing, of that
which I'm bringing more to the plate. Fate declares
nothing. I'm singing the gospel of the probable
scripture. A child once lost, at the costs for all things
worldly. Hurriedly I run to my father. Not to bother
but to make, the things I did take, right. Sight in my
beginnings, did lend me no comfort. My new shirt
will once again, be put on. One gone for the bleeding,
yet shrieking, a new arrival. My bible from God will
decrease the odds, of failure. No fishing lure will
persuade me to do different. I repent for my wrongs
so this song, can have a new tune. The moon is my
guidance, for new scents of joy. Though coy it is all,
the fall, of the fallen. Now rising is the surprising,
comeback. Not new slack but new work, will irk
those of a hurting spirit. Let's hear it for the victor.

For now restored is the board, on which this new game is played. Delayed in its timing, the rhyming of a new rap, will be made. Paid is the homage, of astonished new looks. It took me some time, but now is the sign for a new start. It is the choice, for a better future.

Faith

What is faith? Is it the thought of what life ought to
be? Or is it to see a new concept of our inept ability
in order to overcome the problems in life. A knife is
too sharp but the art of avoiding them relies on our
beliefs. Although brief are the times we get poked,
what's invoked from this is a whist of understanding.
What seems demanding everyday will give way;
but only to those who oppose their own faith. Are
we always safe? No. We still get hurt and pervert
what's right in our lives. Yet, to strive in anything,
you must know faith is a necessary factor. It's the
attractor of well being. It's seeing in the air, what
would appear, not to be there; but to be fair, that's
what makes it all the more appealing. It's feeling
your way through a maze, blind; but to find what
your own heart truly does seek. Though meek is the
journey, the turning point of it all starts with your
faith. It's what makes you great. To relate this to
anything else would be hopeless. Only the soulless
do not have faith. You must trust through the bust, or
busting disappointments life throws at you. All your
food must contain a steady domain of hope. No rope
can hold you back from the slack, or slacking desires
we all have. Pave the path to your own happiness.
In order for all of this to take place you must always
remember, that you undoubtedly do, need faith.

Never Give Up

Giving up is too easy. It's harder to barter for a
better deal. Some feel however, that there are certain
situations giving proclamation to the necessity
of giving up. Well my friends, that just isn't true.
Through my own trials I defiled the many chances
given to me for success. It caused a mess I must
confess, but stopping was never an option. It's a
rotten idea for those who feel their dreams can't come
to life. Their strife has gripped them for disciplines
of unfairness have stricken their minds. They find
themselves victims of systems they cannot control.
Their soul gets weak and does squeak at the thought
that one day everything might be better. Have you
ever tethered this line? Its fine if you have cause this
path is one which is very often traveled. We're baffled
at some of the things life does seem to throw at us.
Yet, it is a must that we continue on. Don't pawn your
soul for something negotiable in a different term. Yes,
you'll have to earn your way to having better days,
but it's worth the trouble. You are doubled with a new
amount of wisdom. It seems dumb at first to thirst for
a while, when there is water right by your side. But
if denied, you'll learn more about yourself. What's
felt in these "friends" can suspend your growth for
greatness. A test is some who come into your life.
And though many let you down you can't frown when
looking life in the face. Know that grace is with you.

Its in who you are as a person. So despite all this nonsense and messed up stuff, you should never say enough is enough. You should never in this lifetime, give up.

Overcoming Problems

We all have problems to overcome. We keep inside
what we decide no one else needs to see. Never free or
relieved, what we believed we could keep to our self
ultimately harms our health in some way. Maybe not
today but tomorrow, when our deepest sorrows come
to the surface. The purpose of this is not to scare you.
It's to get you through some of the most important
times in your life. To strive means to demean the
things so keen on causing your destruction. The
deduction it causes gives rawness to our very self.
Wealth and power will devour us if we don't solve
our true problems. All of them stem from the root. So
what does rot your fruit? Is it the truth in the booth
that causes despair? Is it a snare of your past that does
cast a moment of anxiety upon you? We recruit these
thoughts on a daily basis. For the cases come upon
us that causes us to soon trust wrongful dimensions.
The suspension of this fear makes it clear what we
must do. We must attack these problems head on.
Farther gone will they appear for in the rear they will
disappear from sight. The might it takes to make an
effort to get help is enough. For the stuff born from
nothing bares something in timely fashion. To ration
your blessings means messing with a solution to
whatever problem you are facing at the time. I only
mean to remind you of one thing. Though it is never
fun, we all have our problems that we must, overcome.

Independence

What's it truly mean to be independent? Clearly, we all need help to deal with what's dealt in our hand. No stance can change this. But do we dismiss those who say they did it on their own? What is known is their success but they bless us in showing how anything is achievable. Though unbelievable it may seem that they have done so much. They seem clutch in everything they do. But what's true is something different. They sent for a higher calling by enthralling their minds in their own timely work. They afforded their talents by working so gallantly long on things which belonged to the fundamentals. It's simple really. What you do a million times will give sign to the birthplace for greatness. No messiness can shade what is clear in their results. Their thoughts are in the world to curl the pearling perspective of people being selected into their fields. They yield to a deeper meaning of being what it takes and making the necessary mistakes along the way. They say to the future that their sweat will be the cure to a lazy mindset. Don't take this as a threat to your own beliefs. Just conceive of this as being a perfect idea. So to be honest, the promise to success lies somewhat in your mission to find your own, independence.

Free

It does cost a lot to be free. You can see a happy face
but the race they are running may be far from done.
They may have won in looks, but how do they feel?
Is appeal their concern, or have they learned that
its inner beauty that matters? Do they scatter at the
thought of the Jordan's not bought on time? By now
you should know that there's no room to grow with
possessions. The selection for solutions lie in the
retribution for letting go. It shows your needs aren't
mixed with the greed of this world. The pearl brings
a diamond to those who stop mining for gold. The
treasure essentially, lies within us. It's the trust in our
strengths that drive us to different lengths of success.
We are blessed because the blessing lies dormant in
our pressing souls. So the goal is to dig deep. Keep
your thoughts right and a bright, or brighter future lies
ahead of you. The truth lies within you. You have the
key to simply, set yourself free.

The Quick Night

The nights are going by quick. Each day is proving longer, but the nights; they seem to go by quickly. Now essentially, this was not so. They were very slow due to the fact that not many acts were portrayed on my part; because, I had no plans. The demands for hard work seemed to irk my very soul. I had no intention of doing meaningless labor. Fate does favor the death of the smallest pest of ant work, at least in my mind. It's a kind gesture, but for me, well . . . I'm looking for more out of my life. Maybe a kite-full adventure to the center of the mysterious places on this Earth. Hearing about the Bermuda Triangle gave birth to this idea. The joyous occasion of the oddest persuasion seems to be the most invigorating thing to me. I like to see these mysteries for myself. Not for my health's sake, but simply because they relate something new. Not confused with the conundrum of the sounds that this simple life's drum does seem to repeat. I never retreat from a great journey. My spirit's yearning to see new things and experience what brings a calamity of peace, to me. This can only happen with a plan. I searched for advice as to a wise yet fun adventure, from those around. With a frown they did ask, why the tedious task of this nature would be necessary? Very contrary is the explanation but the sensation for such a trip would give me energy. You see, dreary are the thoughts

of the lost or the weak minded. I'm not saying I'm
either, but I do find an inclined ability to clarify
what life might be trying to hide. There's a lot we
don't know or life simply doesn't show, at least not
as much as others may think. A sink may hold the
water but what bothers me, is what the murky water
doesn't allow me to see. So like a pool, I must dive
in. Within this confinement I will cause a realignment
and reinvent, or discover, something I did not know
before. "To explore is to live," I've always said. So
let my exploration begin. I'll start with a walk down
the bulk, or bulky streets near my house. No mouse
lives in this world without seeing one or two pearls
around it. Meaning this, because it's such a small
creature, it's bound to find features that are amazing,
every day. So with this sway phrase, I will shift my
perspective to that of a mouse. I look for new objects
throughout the Projects of this city. Ha! I'm kidding.
But I will open my gaze to the amazing beauty of
this place. In a walking pace I will notice what has
long went unnoticed. Perhaps a Lotus flower will
catch my eye, causing me to cry for its simplistic
nature. Highly doubtful, but I will take special notice
to certain things. So what do I see? Well, there is
snow that seems to glow so bright. It's practically the
light this very day does need. Almost seems greedy
that it shines brighter than the sun at this moment.
What proponents could cause this? True bliss, never
seems to miss its mark. What else is there? Well, the

air is frigidly cold, proving bold to be the wind as it tries to knock me down. I have to say, today was not the best day to take a walk. I've talked to a couple strangers, which to say the least, was interesting. One did sing a faithful tune on how a full moon would appear tonight. That can't be right. He probably made the song up. The other, was a girl of my age. Paige, I believe her name was. There was a bus she had to catch, but seeing she was a catch of her own, I asked her for a number. With a slumbering reply, a sly smile came across her face. She said with grace, the simple sweetest, but most depleting at certain time word; "Sure." Maybe it wasn't that bad of a day to take a walk. She typed it in my phone and did postpone me from my walk, but then on I went. Time well spent if I do say so myself. What was left of this most exciting journey, you might ask? Well let me take the time to tell you. I walked on through a passage of a tunnel, that led to a bridge. The fridge of God could not demonstrate how cold it was, but I walked on. Noticing rivers, I did deliver a slight glance to see what was in them. As cold as it was, there simply laid still, a white covered dove. Showing its own love for nature, it simply sat there; observing its surroundings. It looked up to my eyes and gave what seemed a simple sigh. Almost as if to say that it tired of each day, when a person of my nature did stare. What a shameful remark. Clearly, this overdressed pigeon was full of itself, so I continued on. Gone was the

chill from this eerie weather. Together, nature and I
seemed to form a compromise. I'd tell no lies of its
beauty so that it would see to my pleasure, of not
freezing. Along this new path I saw half of a gallantly
tall tree. Why only half though? The row, in which
it was split, seemed fit to show it was right down the
middle. This surely has never been seen. No lean to
its own gains, it still remained in all senses of the
phrase, standing tall. Squirrels and raccoons seemed
to move along its halfway formed branches. In their
stances, they did not seem afraid. So I simply waved
so they could relay the message to the rest of their
friends. I began to leave the spot when a thought
soon came to mind. Just maybe it's truly daily that
these occurrences do take place. Not to lay waste
to the human imagination, but I believe if you were
stationed in the same spots I was, you would see the
things I too, did see. You would hopefully continually
remind others that nature has a lot to show, when you
simply take the time to look. Being a man of thought,
what I took from this journey was more. Not to bore
you, but think of this. What if when we are failing
to make our dreams come true, an alternative route
is being formed, right below our eyes? We're busy
seeing failure while our life is showing the future
that we truly desire. The outlier simply is, ourselves.
Even wealth and money does seem to hide and deny
us access to see what life has in store for you and me.
Maybe success relies on the progress we make daily,

but never take the time to see because our inner vision is out of focus. Simply said, maybe we do not say we are great; because innately we do not feel as if we are. To spar with our inner mind is not enough. You must fight it daily, and win; if not at least most of the time. With these signs we will have inner peace. And once inner peace is released, we do have a great sleep. With great sleep our nights dare not make a peep. When our nights do this they do dismiss themselves, causing the night to simply, go by quick.

Insight: The Longest Run

My dad and I were talking the other day. He told me how he would ride his bike for miles and miles for exercise but, he decided he was going to do something different that day. He said, "I'm going to go run the reservoir today." So, I kind of just sat there and said, "Good luck. Have fun. I'll see you when you get back." He said, "No, I want you to come with me. I want you to come run the reservoir with me." Every fiber in body screamed "NO!", but for some reason I said "Okay sure, why not." When we got there we walked for a little bit. I had actually gotten so comfortable with the walking part that I forgot he wanted to run. Out of nowhere he said, "Are you ready?" I just said, "Sure. Let's go."

I remember we rounded the corner and I just thought to myself, "There's no way I'm going to make it all the way around this thing." My dad was trying to talk the whole time during the run, while I was trying to focus on not passing out. It got to a point where I decided, "You know what. I'm not going to keep focusing on how long it takes to actually run the reservoir. I'm going to at least try to engage in this conversation."

We ended up talking about everything including stocks and sports; just everything. Before I knew it we were almost at the end. I realized I had more energy at that time than ever before. We ended up seeing my mom walking the track. My dad said, "You go ahead, I'll walk back with your mom." I said, "Okay." I kept jogging. It looked like I had at least a mile left, and I decided, "You know what, why not just get this over with?" I started jogging faster and faster. It got to a point where I was at a full out sprint.

At the end my parents seemed amazed because they didn't think I had that much energy left. What they didn't realize was that the reason I did finish (and didn't pass out in the middle of it) was because our whole conversation took my mind off of the jog. When I got home I sat there for a second and realized something. In life, it's not about how long the race is; but, how much of the race you can actually enjoy.

CHAPTER 4

Chapter 4: Beliefs

It's very important to believe in something. It defines your character and keeps you consistent. My beliefs on life use to change every time I heard what other people said. Nothing changed for me until I came up with my own beliefs. However, they may be formed in different ways. My personal beliefs came from experience. Sharing beliefs can also help in the forming process. Having your own beliefs also helps in the forming of your own attitude towards life. These next writings deal with just that; beliefs. Some of them mention my personal experiences, how I came to form most of them, and what I witnessed in order to do so.

Believe

It's always important to believe. Even in my lowest
moments I honed in on a certain belief. It's hard to
realize that the skies, or sky, is the limit. Many times
we find certain limitations put on us by others. And
if you believe them, no friend can mend all the scars
to come next. Yet if we believe for more, we sore to
newer heights. Of course there will be newer fights
and more devious plights, but you'll be alright in
the end. Our fears somehow, even now, can stop this
from happening. It's no mystery that we must be
bold in the old but very well told story that you can
be and achieve anything you believe to be yours.
The only thing that can be taken away from you is
belief in the truth of yourself. If you only think little
of what brittle mindset you have, you will never
achieve anything. Sometimes you have to know and
grow in what is a true fact; you create your own
future. Now don't get me wrong, no song is ever
sung in perfect pitch. Some squeaks and mistakes
will always be there to take your motivation. It's an
invasion we call discouragement. But don't descend
from what lies within you. You have a calling that's
sprawling at the thought of coming out. If only you're
willing to believe. Deceit is also a treat sent from the
enemy. This is meant to persuade and degrade you
as a person. With perfect belief you can keep this
from happening. Your dreams need to seem, or see,

a fighting chance. So take stance in a battle that will rattle even your deepest fears. Make sure to stay near to the sincere thought, that what's sought in your soul requires a bold action. You must believe.

Insight: Foreseen Miracles

I had just received confirmation that I got the job. It was exciting because you rarely can get a job being fresh out of college; though some think otherwise. It was only a part time job at this company. I was in training, getting use to how things were going to work and seeing what to expect. I had no idea of the changes that were about to be made. On the second week of training we were all notified that the department was shutting down.

You hear so much about company lay-offs, but you never think it will actually be your company (that recently gave you the job) that would do so. I had no idea what I was about to do. Should I try to find another job? Should I look for a job inside the company? Should I even stay with a company that was implementing lay-offs? My decision was shortly narrowed down.

The company decided they were going to keep as many people as they could, but there were no guarantees that you would get the job. My odds were very slim, being a new hire and all. We had 60-days to choose if we were going to stay with the company or look for another job. A lot of people ended up moving and taking the severance package. People who had worked there for years and years were all of the sudden being forced out of a job. It was a sad day for the company and the people who worked in it.

If you walked into the office you could tell it was a close-knit family. People would walk from desk to desk talking about life and everything in-between. There was no hierarchy; the manager wasn't above a supervisor, a supervisor wasn't higher than a lead, and the lead wasn't hire than the representatives. They were all respective of the departments and the other departments around them. The perfect office if you ask me.

But, I had a decision to make. I could either stay with the company, or endure tedious interviews with other companies who had no intentions of hiring me. I ended up choosing to stay, though everyday I'd hear "there's a slim chance you'll get the job" or "if I were you, I'd be looking for a new job". I tried to maintain focus and keep working, but I have to admit, some of it got to me.

It came down to the last week, and being the only one not notified of the job offering, I kept working. All my friends in training got the job and were planning for the future with the company. It didn't seem to help being focused and as diligent as I could possibly be.

Doubts crept up on the last three days. I decided to stick with the company even though the future of it seemed very meek. I'd go home staying awake, thinking about what the future had planned for me. Sometimes I'd have nightmares where everybody in the world got the job, while I was packing my things, heading out of the building. It seems like a lot of unnecessary stress for just getting hired on as a part-time worker right?

The very last day I was notified that I had gotten the job, but not just any job. It was THE job. It was a full-time, career-starting, upper-level type of job. It came with benefits; free this, free that, and an all-expense-paid vacation. Turns out that what they say is true. Miracles do not happen without belief.

What They're Saying

I'm starting to understand what they're saying. They
might complain as much as a campaigning bunch of
politicians, but I understand. Scrambling to see or
even bring any truth to light. Yet they fight without
sight, using all their might, just to delight themselves,
but nobody else. Always instigating a situation
without the delegation or true justification through
their own reprimanding rights. They are crooked;
sideways folks with jokes, who never seem to listen,
but poke fun at the ones who had once spoke. Oh tell
me when they'll stop so the plot of those who are not
these politicians will come to see true Christians and
others with wisdom, will soon take lead. Not to lay
greed or incept the need for power. But to shower the
people of this great nation with truth. Now, I'm not
saying religion will plow the seeds for the cows with
no respective beliefs. But what leaks, will be the peak
of what will become known as the greatest shown
glory. So it's true, I'm starting to understand what
they're saying. Playing the fool will get you trust but
making the choice to seek lust will end in total failure.
But what will you say to these people speaking every
day? Will you rise above and show love to even those
you once hated? Or be delegated to those related to
the unjust that should've been, but were never sedated
by the real truth? Because they didn't accept the
truth. But rather stayed and played with the ideas of

others, from calling one another brother so that it's
no wonder why they came to the realization of hate.
Just don't be late to the fact that to communicate with
these persons will do you no good. In choosing other
ways one day you can say you followed your own
true beliefs. So when that time comes you can sit back
and hum, "my beliefs make me, truly, who I am",
even though, I'm starting to understand what they're
saying.

A Sudden Change

As time moves on I start to see,

That people change so suddenly.

Their choice is made for good or bad,

And then they leave to then be sad.

It could just lead to changing clothes,

Or how they look to different roles.

The point in which is that their change,

May cause their life to rearrange.

The order though they keep in mind,

That once they change they don't rewind.

They don't look back though some regret,

The things they've done to stay content.

Their needs all gone no more control,

They've left that life to keep their soul.

Yet still there is a piece of them,

That won't let go but still defend.

What it feels right and what is wrong,

To make the change still far from gone.

But this in fact may change all lives,

So that this one still has to strive.

For different fits will move on down,

Their newborn lives where they don't frown.

Instead they see a greater light,

In which they know they've won the fight.

So once it's done they feel simply,

That now they'll live their life freely.

Please Take A Deeper Look

Please take a deeper look. I don't know if he was
shook by the drama, or maybe the sauna of heat from
the weather. For better or worse I hope he comes
out of this comatose state of mind. So blind to the
gathering of awkward yet devious things that did
bring him to this point. To anoint another source of
this cause would simply be false. Stating that through
mandating or delegating the nuance of problems had
been nothing but bad and the cause of his sad health.
Seeking wealth, he found it fit to quit the occupations
of sensational enjoyment; all for the employment
of money. Whether rainy or sunny he would be at
work. Not with a smirk, but a jerk from side to side
with true pride that lost the fight for him on this
day. In dismay of the abysmal amounts of tasks not
completed he deleted the one thing he needed; his
self. For the realm of the Spirit is deciphered by those
who feel it in themselves. Yet he put all emotions
away to complete the problems at bay; simply, trying
to find the solution. No institution denies what he
did to confide in due time, to be wrongful thinking.
Though gone now, I must say he did know how to
find the answer. He'd search through the mountains
and test every fountain; just to taste the truth. Yet,
the youth in him was instinctual. Through believable
events he did represent himself as being pleasantly
fine. Though confined to his own confusion, he ended

up leaving loose ends in his money seeking life.
So here he is presently. Not able to move or see, he
simply lies on this destitute ground. Those who are
now around reading this sound doctrine of truth, I ask
you to do one thing. Step back from life's tease of
money and ease and PLEASE, take a deeper look.

Free Your Mind

Free your mind. Is it really that hard of a concept?
To be inept in your ability to pick or choose what
you will refuse to let in your head? Think instead
of it like this; dismiss the hate and separate your
dreams from nightmares. Impaired vision brings a
collision but not with the mind. You find the more
that it stores the more you implore your intelligence.
And since intelligence is relevance you must sense
your surrounding walls. Through these walls you
install your own protection and provide reflection to
guide you. What's true for you is never true for others
because no mind bothers to see viewpoints from eye
to eye. The lies to one are truths in which cover the
stuttering effects of every event you pertain to. So to
conclude this interlude of confusion, make a provision
to see things differently. Think clearly for what you
believe is necessary for your life. Don't get right with
others until you fight the smother of problems in you.
Recruit help to make your mental health to the best of
its capable nature. And be pure to sign with the idea
of freeing your mind.

The Light Shines Bright

The light shines bright. Even in my darkest hours the power to see the light resides in me. Fearing what's in my future I tutor the thoughts of everything being in God's hands. His plan overcomes the things I've not done in my own life, to make better strides. What pride is this? To cause my bliss to leave where I can only believe the change will arrange fame in the right order? My borders, or walls, have fallen so I can rebuild. Yet still, it's not as easy as it looks. What I took from this idea is to be a great state of confidence. No senses tell me that, but giving slack to how it was back in the day; it tells me to stay on this path. No wrath can stop me. I'm free from the burdens of things that were hurting my soul. I was bold in cutting this unnecessary pain off. No trough to eat from, I became one with my inner Spirit's conscious. No nuances can take from my mistakes; but I'll make it. Never one to quit I'll move along to better songs that tune my wrong strings together. Though the weather brings a dark night, my might helps me to know; the light indeed, does shine bright.

Small Lights Confine No One

Small lights confine no one. Everyone's defined
by the things they intertwine with in life. Whether
it's taking the knife out of the back of friends who
have slacked in being honest, or even promising to
help when the health of others are declining. We're
signing our lives to strive for better things. So when
the shine is not what you thought it'd be simply
think, did I sink into darkness or leave the lawless
behavior behind? Never mind that right now, for
even cows bow down to sound judgment. Reluctant
to understand the causation for curiousness is easy;
sleep freely in the thoughts of the unknown. What's
grown from ideas brings a fear of the plain signs.
The paradigms where nothing seems to change and
the pain grows to a point where even the fixed man's
joints must be adjusted. A gruesome thing does
not bring me to say this; you truly can have bliss.
Through the chains holding back how you never
chose to act; yet, you can still rise higher. Like a
fire growing tall, the walls of defeat lay at your feet.
Demonstrations across the nations will show you
how many have achieved what was once believed
impossible. But don't take your hand off that throttle.
Go full speed till you feel the need to stop. You are
in control of your life. Don't believe the lies from
the eyes of those who haven't seen anything. Trust
that your actions will give a reaction for a promising

tomorrow; simply borrow these positive intuitions for the mission isn't yet complete. Let me show you what's really true for all of us. Never seeing the truth leaves you trapped in a loop through which no man can escape. Be the planet, not the ape, who takes control. Remote signs of greatness related to safeness do not exist. You don't need bright lights to give might to your talents. So with that I rather show some, that small lights confine no one.

Closer Friends

These un-assuring times, show the mind's delicacy.
Every day we try to retrieve what we believe will help
us later on. So far gone are the options of what can
truly help and what tends to hurt us. We try not to fuss
about our mistakes, but what we take is not a lesson.
We regress when we fight and complain, knowing that
each domain has been corrupted, in our soul. We hold
dearly, what sincerely was meant to help us. Yet, each
day gives a new say to how our future will be shaped.
We tape our concerns to what we do learn, throughout
each of our experiences. However, don't let this
scramble of words bring discernment to what you've
earned when, you had nothing to gain. Learn to be
what you want, without being to blunt in your actions.
It's not the reaction that brings worry, but what's
buried in our inactiveness will eventually, come to
life. There is no such thing as good strife. Everyday
what tends to stress us will never bless, but instead,
will do just the opposite. It will cause pain when the
sane mind knows better. Each day we experience new
weather, regardless of our needs. Yet, we proceed to
do what has to be done. Fun is an action that never
seems to ration how we should live our life. Each day
should be a blessing, even in the times of our testing;
when we do feel like we'll fail. Hail to the King, who
does bring us hope; yet, knows no dictatorship. It is
relationships that hold us together. Even when we

tether between the lines of, winning and losing our mind it's, the people around us who hold us down. They seem to be around at the right, exact moments. It's the proponent that weighs the balance of each day that we see them. Believe them when they say that, "everything will be better." So remember to keep a friend who will send the right message. Positivity brings no proclivity to what initially, needs to be done. We tend not to take the first step unless there's somebody giving us the push to do so. Know that your success is no less than what the people around you say it will be; and eventually, you'll see that even in these unassuring times we can find solace. We can thrive in this lively world.

Be Honest

Just be honest. Through my life all strife came from lies. They caused pain and little gain to myself and to others. I can only imagine, what others were trying to fathom from the things I had said. Never led, but leading them to true despair, I cast all cares aside. Simply to glide on my own pride and nothing else. From this my soul felt wrong, so along came a reawakening. I was beginning to tell the truth. I didn't want people to feel the things I deal with when I'm hurt. To flirt with those kinds of things only brings sadness. So when the madness of lies stop, the rot you feel soon leaves. Breathe in now clean air for the sharing of truths brings happiness. For gladness the stakes are high but with each lie we are brought down. Not simply to the ground but to be pounded beneath the soil. Don't let the turmoil of lies bring you to this state. Instead, negate the desire to be called a liar and rise above so the ones who love you see who you really are. So far is the soul that low and beholds no right. For the might of each lie does cut down the lives of others in the worse way. I beg this thought stays in your mind so as you rewind back to this, you will remember. Not the tender way it was said but instead remember the importance of it all. The call for true statements relate that being honest truly does bring promise to a clearer conscious mindset. No regret from the past will last or show contest; just as long as you choose to be honest.

Depend on God

Right now I'm just debating what to do. There are choices with voices trying to attract me. I can see this will not be done with ease. Do I please myself by remaining the same? Or do I have something to gain from making some minor changes? There's no guarantee in either. I've always been a seeker of success but what's best for right now has escaped my mind. I'm not blind but its dark, for the ark in my decision gives me no leniency. Dependently I do wait to hear what God has to say. My decision does sway depending on his path. It's not his wrath that I'm afraid of, but help from above has always been sought out through my nature. Only a failure to notice this could bring me to my demise. So the skies, in essence, have the answer. Though the cancer causing my indecision is still here. I only fear I won't be able to decipher what he's saying. I'm praying for the day where I can say I've got life figured out. But I doubt that will happen. To simply fathom the fact that these problems are not here to stay, simply brings peace to my conscious. What it all seems to boil down to is dependence. No recompense does send a sense to rely on one's self. It's the health of the Lord that does afford me during these times. So I'll look for a sign and keep in mind, that I must, depend on God.

The Selection of Rejection

True words were spoken today. While waiting around, I found something out, from a good friend of mine. He said, "Handling rejection is the reflection of one's true character." Not only was this well-worded, but if blurted out by anyone else, it would not have been received. I conceive of this belief because what he does, well, it deals with a lot of ups and downs. Turnarounds are unlikely and as frightening as it is to believe in yourself, he maintains a level of success. But let's digress from him as a person and focus on rejection. Let's face it, rejection sucks. It plucks us out individually, and remedies everything we believe to be good in ourselves. Whether its talking to a girl, or giving a whirl to a new business idea, rejection is bound to follow. It's the pain and the sorrow of "feeling" not good enough. I must admit, it is hard to get over this. But what if you dismissed rejection as being a negative thing? For instance, bring rejection to its lowest form. If the norm for you is to go on through the easy path, simply because rejection is too much, try facing it head on. It's gone within minutes, when seen fit to be under your own control. If you talked to five ladies, there's maybe at least two that will give you their number. And isn't that the goal? So what if the three reject you? You still found true selection between two others. That is what determines success. Finding best, in bad situations, that there is one who also decided to choose you. Who needs thousands of companies, when one does seem to make you a billionaire? You don't need all the women when one then can make you feel like you're on top of the world. It's really basic knowledge that even college kids seem still to forget. But in retrospect, rejection is simply a sign that's design was meant to weed out the weak. Don't seem so meek when it arises, its disguise is meant to bring you success. Be select in this sentimental theory, and eerie is the mystery of which your greatest results will come. It's only your neglection to choose rejection as being harmful. Truthfully, you will see, rejection is a good thing.

Responsibility Is a Must

Responsibility is a must. Everybody's responsible
for the probable things in life. What they like does
strike a concern in their very conscious. Without it
sound doubts fit the mold of whatever reflecting and
ever rejecting thought process they have. Does this
wrath continue? Simply issue a new brain to those
waning in pain from the whole ordeal. We do feel
sorry for these happenings going on. Yet, know your
mind. Is it kind to positive thoughts or is it bought by
what's entertaining? Is it staining your perspective on
things which seem selective in your present living?
Maybe giving you relief to uncertain beliefs causing
stress? We all know this happens. The dissonance
in our cognition gives suspicion to what we have
to deal with. The pith of this world does curl our
vivacious imagination. Change the station when this
occurs. Don't be blurred by wrong sightings that
seem so delighting at the moment. Just own it. This
way we give a huge amount of trust, in knowing,
responsibility is a must.

Secrets to Wealth

There are secrets to wealth. It provides a somewhat
guide in our life. Knowing what's growing in our
bank accounts does amount to a very pleasing feeling.
Though, is that wealth? Maybe the stealth of money
isn't funny to others, but it is to me. To see what new
fads make people glad does catch my interest. Yet
tempers flare when the glares of others are not upon
them. Maybe insecurity has been found but for now
I have a different meaning for this. It's to find bliss,
for that is what wealth truly is. Not the gist of new
cars or buying the bar completely out. It's a stout
reminding of finding what intrinsically motivates you.
It's the truth that we seek to peak in whatever we find
interestingly relevant to our minds. Be it kindness
and joy to employ others and giving brothers a new
outlook on life, or maybe healing the feeling of never
being enough. In everything we can bring ourselves
wealth. You simply have to look at what was took, or
taken from you that you miss. To dismiss what you
need will cause greed and rejection from the election
of all morale behavior. Let your savior guide and help
rely on the good word. Do not let your pleasures be a
must or measures of lust will fill your spirit. Hear it
well and do dwell on the great things your blessings
have given you. With this you'll find stealth and great
health, because there truly are, great secrets to wealth.

Work Defines Us

The work we do defines us. Never-mind the simple signs of test and exams. What we do daily defines us. The bust in this is what we dismiss to call work. Work is a task that reveals the mask of our true character. Whether rare at first, we show what we conceive to believe through our work. So what is work? Is it the job that never lobs you a chance at success? Or is it the mess you have fixed that betwixt your very capability of reading a manual? I do think it's the brink of genius. It's what we devote in a thing that gives us hope to ring a resounding yell for satisfaction. The reaction of course is labor and force that we must individually conceal to see the future at hand. It demands of our time but declines the notion in which it needs. We proceed this path because our passion gives wrath to failure. In essence, we do it all as a choice. We're not commanded to grow in a field we do know, with no promise. And to be honest, we do not know the positive effects beforehand. Some of us might just find delight in moving forward with our work. We know it's hard but disregard this fact. It does last pass our past to bring us a greater prospect. The effect in this ripple does triple what it cost in seed. No greed will need to intercede the outcome. What's done is done, regardlcss or not if it was fun in the end. To this I remind that the work in which we do. It does, define us.

Satisfaction

Are we ever truly satisfied? I find it hard to believe,
that we ever truly, are satisfied. With no guide to
confide in, we must realize when our needs are met.
Sometimes the guilt, of money that's spilt, proves to
remind us of something. What's the one thing that we
truly want? No blunt thing can answer this question.
It takes reflection upon the mind to show sign of our
true heart's desire. There's a fire in all of us that we
must trust to understand our own plan's demand in the
depth of our core. It is to restore and lay rest to our
needy pest of an idea that we need more to be happy.
The sappy romance gives stance to this foundation.
The derogation for this ground proves sound in
judgment, but not in heart. For the art of being truly
satisfied lies in your own creativity. The activity
brings such feeling that we must sing for we all are, in
our own soul. The toll of this knows no bliss does last
forever. But regardless of the weather no happiness
is severed through hard times. They are mimes in
our lives; standing quietly they wait to see when
you will notice them to be there. Not so fair is the
unjust though no fuss makes living an adventure. Just
to ensure you know, all seeds will grow in season.
This is the reason we may or may not be, ever truly
satisfied.

Empathy

Are you empathetic to this life? Do you understand
the strands that attach together through every
opportunity? No one has purity but simply, a
good heart. It's the start to all right intentions. The
suspension of wrong actions seem to fraction out
the greatest personality. What's sad, you see, turns
out to be what is overlooked. The booked sensation
from having no relation to that person brings a new
gap. One that caps the lid and gets rid of any hope.
So, are you really empathic to this life? All strife and
mayhem brought from us and maybe them, happens
accidentally. Ironically, we can only hope for a better
tomorrow. All our sorrow must subside while our
God does guide our movement. There are angels sent
on both sides for us to rely on, on a daily basis. New
faces bring us joy but to employ this new outlook we
must see whose rook has been taken. Not mistaken,
we must go where they know we don't want to be.
Symmetry seems right but in plain sight we know
both sides won't match. That's the catch. What's right
will not always look right. All fights don't need all
our true might, and all plights of a mysterious plot,
never do seem to take flight till the end. What sends
us our desire to inspire others? I'm sorry for the party
of philosophical thought. But you ought to think on
these things to give meaning to your daily life. So
never regret it, simply be empathetic to this life.

A New Mind

What's a new day without the fade of past events? A
new mind gives hint to what's meant to begin each
morning. Though boring is the start of lost art, in
which we try to make together. Forever it is clever
to see something that will ring a new bell for us all.
Never dull is the problem though stationary solvents
demote our ambitious ways. Our gaze becomes fixed
in one direction. The selection as to what is right still
remains somewhat of a mystery. History shows us
through wrongful lust a disgusting amount of evil
that has been done. All because the passionate fun
we once had has slid away. Only now our dismay in
knowing what's growing can help us to dissolve this
unfulfilling taste . . . .

I'm sorry. I hope this didn't confuse you. What I'm
trying to say is each day we must start with a new
mind. It inclines the rebel and brings a new level to
our accomplishments. It gives the scent of success.
Just reminisce in that thought. We brought ourselves
from certain hells, for what? To live in mediocrity?
No, though Socrates did have one famous quote. He
was remote to say this, "the only true wisdom is in
knowing you know nothing." This does bring me
satisfaction. The reaction to this is to slowly dismiss
all past knowledge. Not to be dumb but to hold a
thumb to that opened door. Know that more is great,

and helps to relate us to our successful ancestries.
You aren't the tease but the key to an ever-growing
tree for the future. This is something you must realize
individually. For if you see this, true bliss can't miss
in meeting your path. Never laugh at what's unknown
for a grown man even loses the will to understand the
most basic foundations of wisdom. Never succumb
to these problems, but in solving them arise to a new
height. Your flight is yours alone, a king to your own
throne you must be. Free is the mind that is kind to
untactful things. So with this thought to stay, you
must know that each day, you must find, a new mind.

What's There to Say?

What's really left to say? Some days I ask this; to
dismiss an action helps some relax when they are
tense. Not so much for me. When I'm angry to the
moment, where no proponent can calm me down, I
just think; is this going to hurt me? At the end, will
I be mad or just sad? When I think on this I tend to
do the right thing. Out of the things I've faced, I've
never chosen to misplace my goals. Those are the
only bonds holding me together. I never forget my
purpose. It's no to surface as a star, but simply to
go far, and also to different lengths; simply, to bring
strength to those who think they are weak. Meek
are their thoughts, when they ought to know the
truth. Proof comes from actions, where satisfaction
meets actuality. No legality makes this a law, but
like a saw, it helps to cut out what's not needed.
Pleaded in a guilty case, few do waste their time in
a meaningless chase for glory. "Be the story," a wise
man said. Laid in bed, I thought on his words. Is it
absurd to want the bluntest thing in life? Success?
Yes, it's a test, though the end never begins, we do
send someone to see if there is any red tape. Hoping
to escape this life, their strife is put aside where it
does not confide in anything. Only singing about its
health, and in stealth, is it heard. Only blurred are
the words its trying to pronounce. Separate accounts
are soon charged, to those who do barge in; simply

to say that this day, another man's dream cannot be seen. This is a keen thing I choose to think on. Gone till the end, I do recommend that till then, there is nothing left to say.

Tendencies

It's only normal to have different tendencies. They
are key to successful living but also can bring a
stressful environment. It's kind of meant to get you
leaning in one way. Some days it helps because you
are dealt with a certain motivation to do rightful
actions, though the fraction of your mind does not
want to. It's true either way, but other days they
will be considered bad habits. They indeed, stint
your growth. They loath for destruction and the
corruption they cause leaves an even longer line
of problems. So how do we solve them? How do
we get our tendencies to see what we try to seize
in our daily life? Well, it's simple. The principle is
basic. You do pick the smallest actions to do every
week. At the peak of this foundation a station will
be formed. It's normed, or normal, to want to give
in. Within there's a battle that rattles our own logic.
Nostalgic ideas tend not to leave peacefully. So
recently it was discovered that others have broken
these habits in less then three weeks. Others seek to
find these similar results. A malt or new mix does
fix this pessimistic trick our bad habit did make.
Mistakes do take a lot out of us, but never fear!
It's clear that these problems can be overcome.
They are do e in their making now shaking your
tendencies to lean in the right direction. The
affection, or effect, will be felt shortly after. A new

chapter can be started cause you marketed a better, more improved you. So it's true, though we all have different tendencies, they are ultimately made by you.

Patience

Life truly takes patience. It never makes sense, but to
achieve what we want we must be blunt in waiting.
Though fading in the boredom the unsung truth of
it all is that it doesn't happen in the blink of an eye.
That, in itself, is the biggest lie any person could
possibly tell you. What's felt through waiting is
more important anyways. The thing that stays and
gives say is knowledge. Knowledge of the unknown
that is grown where others choose to ignore it. And
isn't that really the best kind? Rewind on back to a
time where you truly felt smart. Didn't it start with
an astonished look on their face? Its not disgrace by
any means. If anything, it's the praising of the fact
that you told them something they had then, never
realized. Through their eyes you can see that they'll
never forget this moment. That is when you truly felt
the power in the hour of your best choosing. So losing
patience is more or less like losing more moments
in this. In that missed moment of bliss you dismiss a
great thing. You can bring however, these moments
to pass. Wouldn't it last to make some truly great
memories? Few do see this and that is what makes it
so great. We relate the need to feel greed, but don't do
it with this saying. Keep relaying the message to all of
your friends. Only then will your patience be honored.
You should never be anxious, because all you really
need is a fine amount of patience.

Wellness

Things are well. Though swell is the weather I
came to soon tether on the idea of wellness. Not
healthiness, or health should I say, but the changing of
each day seems to bring something good. Understood
is the meaning of being a better person, these changes
are not necessarily affected by my actions. They
seemed to be happening at random. No tandem of
combinations brings the satiable fact that my acts
have brought these new blessings to my life. Though,
I do remember one simple change. It was actually
more of a routine. It never seemed keen to these
results but no cult could argue with this outcome. The
sum of it all does fall upon a decision made a couple
months ago. It was to grow in what I know by saying
what is relaying to my future. It's now pure in thought
to have a clear conscious. Though nonsense at the
time I started speaking to the present time. Aloud
I would say, "I'm the king of this day! No one can
bring me down or cause a frown from this moment
on!" Sounds crazy doesn't it? But it's only fit to tell
you what happened. It's the caption of this moment
that owned it, or better yet said, I owned every dismal
day. As long as I say that phrase the haze from each
problem cleared up. I could solve every puzzle and
win in each rustle the day handed me. It was key for
me to focus on that simple phrase; I'm The King of
This Day. To no dismay each day seemed brighter.

The lighter was on and gone were my pessimistic thoughts. It brought me a new understanding to life. I thrive in what I strive to say, consistently, to each day I am living. In giving my words I did blur the actions of the enemy. Finally I could see how life was meant to be lived. No thrift of the weather could bring more than a feather, or ounce, of doubt. The route to wellness was found. So, deep down I soon dwelled on the thoughts and actions of each day that things are most definitely now, well.

A New Change

The time for change is coming. Well, it's swell to
dwell on the fact that the time is now. How did it
come to this? Are we leaving true bliss to simply
dismiss all good behavior? It's always a favor to
savor the good ole days. Confused and in a daze, we
chose to go with those who go after pleasure. Giving
a feeling that healing has taken place. But in disgrace,
they have caused more damage. We managed to make
a disease that did please the Devil himself. But do
not be alarmed. We were armed for this years ago.
Although, we forgot where we put the weapon. It's
in the section where many truths seem to be lost. The
cost for this is, our Spirit. Endear it to a much higher
calling. The stalling of this nature does cater to more
problems. But, if you find the key and believe the
weapon is real, you'll heal what you believed to be
deadly. Directly does it cause a pause for all selective
wrong that was done. It's not fun; I should definitely
warn you of that. The stats are greater to state how
a fear, can be removed. Abused is this old, yet basic
idea. So, what is one to do? Can we too, cause more
healing than pain? Of course we can! Though the
domain restrains us from accessing it like magic.
It's an experiential type of deal. You must seal your
promise to the honest works that are from above.
Show love to a stranger though anger might come
your way. Stay in the midst of each day; showing your

ray of light can delay any sight, of creeping darkness.
Success is only blessed when considered for the
betterment of man. So do you have a plan? I really do
understand. It's simple in concept though precepts the
context of the ideas from flowing in. We must then
come together. Who said that stormy weather couldn't
tether on the lines of being a blessing? We must bring
all the youth to a wisdom filled booth so they'll learn.
We must earn the trust of others, in which covers
them of their past sin. Give in to forgiveness. Even
though, it's something few can do. Be true in yourself
to go bring health to an unstable mind. Be kind, not
blind, to the actions of people. The prequel to this
story should have a much brighter beginning, with the
ending of this inspiring you. I do choose a better life
for you and me both. The oath from God would also
agree. So do please remember this. That to kiss death
means giving rise to a theft, from an unguarded safe.
He's taken the lock so we could talk about taking this
world back. Give no slack, but do understand that no
one is perfect. Select your battle and do not be rattled,
for this time, truly, is the time for change.

The Prayer

Sitting down today I calmly thought of everything
that's happened. The caption of the moment, "Success
Achieved." I never believed it would come time
where fine dining and wine would take its place in
my life. Yet, that's not what I'm reflecting on. It
dawned on me what did free these blessings upon this
current hour. Never fouler were my mistakes than
they were in my past. But what cast those mistakes
aside? Neither pride nor a simple guide did do the
trick. But maybe, well essentially; it all might have
started with a prayer. In my moment of true despair I
declared to write, and say aloud, a prayer in which I
would say every day. It made way for my confidence
and brought upon me a highly favored self esteem.
To seem clear, it would reappear in my memory. It
simply went something like this. Lord, please dismiss
those whose throes in life did cause them to do harm.
Arm them with a clearer conscious. Please take
away their nauseous behavior, and give them peace.
Lord, please release an unreasoning favor from you,
my Savior, to a more humbling me. Since defeat
has taken its stay, please sway me into believing all
problems can be overcome. Allow one of your angels
to protect me. For reflecting on failure only seems
to bring pain. Lord, ordain success to reminisce in
every aspect I do neglect to deem important. For the
ordinance of my necessity does give plea to a better

understanding of what I need to do. Please bless
those who are confused and did elude them from
their calling. They are crawling when they should
be sprawling at the greatest opportunity; their life.
Please do not trifle with those whose rows are lined
with bad intentions. And also, give extension to
those who wish to do good. And now, what should
I do Lord? I afford your opinion since you have
dominion over my heart. Let me start to do what
was born through the talents you have given me.
Relieve me of the stress all these tests and pests seem
to bring. Sing me a song, or hum along while I sing
the gospels of the almighty things you have already
done. Though I've had fun give me tasks, where
then I will ask more questions, simply for direction
as to where to go next. Help select my new friends
that will send prayers for me, as I for them. Resend
a career that would endear me to increase me as a
person, everyday. Never fade from my sight so I can
delight in your wisdom. Do not let rum or beer be the
common cheer to my saddened days. And for each
maze, please help to guide me through. You are truest
in my darkest hour. Give power for me to then see
the light. Help me fight for others, whom I'll call my
brothers, in their moments of need. Let greed not be
freed in my life; for generosity will forever light my
torch. Let my porch be facing away from the wind,
so I can surely spend these nights and days in peace.
Give feast to the hungry, and clothes to the humbling

homeless souls of this Earth. Rebirth in them a new vengeance to live right. Reunite all my causes to simple clauses, as if my wrongs never took place. Give space between those who do not get along. They belong to a sincerefull mindset. Let all regrets vanish for it famishes the human soul. Give me goals Lord, for I adore meaningful work. Create a circuit in me that gives plea with those who are annoying me, daily. Safely remove the wrongful grooves made in those hurting from pain. Remain a steady friend in their lives. I do believe I have strived for the best in humanity through prayer. Though rare are my actions, I give satisfaction to what has been said. Relinquished of all sin, I do say then; amen. And with that simple prayer, I did layer myself with protection. So as a reflection, my recollection of what brought me to this point, simply came from an anointed, prayer.

CHAPTER 5

Chapter 5: The Future

One of the sayings that always bothered me was, "You have to plan your future." After hearing that all the time in college I still had no real idea how. I use to think, "If you can't predict the future, how are you suppose to plan for it?" Turns out I was wrong. It's not about setting goals that aren't realistic. It's about envisioning what you want your future to be. It's sitting down and taking some time to yourself to think about your dreams. You have to visualize what it would be like to achieve them. This was the starting point for me. The mind is an amazing thing once a dream becomes a realistic achievement. The more you dwell on your dreams the more your life starts to gravitate towards making it happen. Writing this book started out as a dream. I started writing it after one day where I sat down, thought about it, and about what it would be like to be considered an author. And you know what, it was an exciting feeling! Only then did I put pen to paper. Thinking about your future is important to making your dreams come true. The following poems sample futuristic thought. They give an insight into some of the views I had on how I wanted my life to be in the future that also gave me some inspiration.

Your Plan

Take the time you never had,

To build just one thing more.

A song to bring all people close,

That walks them through the door.

Or simply make a moment last,

Where all greatness is found.

That makes a long, lasting effect,

That's felt by all around.

Or maybe stop a problem now,

That hurts you down the way.

Instead create an answer that,

Is found on this new day.

Regardless, try to show the world,

You have something they don't.

A missing piece of the puzzle,

Which others threat but won't.

For they all know you're well in need,

A beauty to their beast.

You bring healing from every side,

And hold the Sorrow's leash.

The power lies only with you,

To keep sadness at bay.

And only you release greatness,

And give all angels say.

I know, I know, you don't think so,

But this, my friend, is true.

The day will not begin until,

Your smile does break through.

You hold the key to victory,

You give life and no sin.

You help create a calming sense,

That spreads to all within.

So do not let the past dictate,

For now you know the truth.

And everything from this day on,

All now belongs to you.

Yes peace, wisdom and happiness,

Are all in your own hand.

So now that you do know all this,

Tell me, what is your plan?

This Is Just The Beginning

This is just the beginning. It was a huge bust to find out what a fuss this did cause. Never applauded but always thought it interesting what would start it all. Would it be the fall of all mistakes or would it take me less than that to get the facts? What an impact this all had on me. To finally see and believe all I needed to achieve great wealth was here all along. Never belonging in different groups I did find a soup I could call my own. One higher than the throne for all to taste rather than simply to give waste to the plain and ordinary. Was it scary? Very much so. But to grow we must trust God. If we're at odds with him then the simplest form of sin can ruin it. Yet even I made this all fit to happen. With me being my own captain I had to start somewhere. Just with care and no luck I became very stuck in seeing what this blessing was doing in my life. I made it a custom to relieve the strife of others because even brothers have to help one another out. This way they don't doubt what they were made for. To travel to places never seen before in the glory of telling a story that just so happened to be true. And through it we find something. Rustling through the junk we finally find the trunk of treasure. Yet what can we use to measure the loot? The fruit of our labor has finally helped us to conceive of a newfound satisfactory type of notion. The kind causing commotion throughout society but the propriety of what was sought could never be bought; it can only be achieved through a thorough search. What will emerge will bring you to your knees, yelling "Oh please Lord, let me never afford to lose such a beauty of a prospect." And with respect you'll show it off until the clearing of a cough helps you to understand. All of this was not part of the plan. Your demand for others to feel jealous of what zealous diamond-in-the-rough type thing you received. You breathed in the fresh air and lost all despair through your findings. Did you not sing the joys of it after? Of course you did, simply to capture the moment. And no postponement of this evening could ever soon bring you to this conclusion; which is, this is all just the beginning.

I Can See Success

I can see success. It's true, out of the blue and
also through my dreams I'm starting to see it. I'm
beginning to fit into the mold of success in which I
was blessed and destined to join. No coin could flip
and predict this. I must admit, I did dismiss this idea.
An idea in which the switch would be flipped up to
the point where I would suddenly anoint my gifts.
The gifts that did shift my perception. In reflection
I've found this new doctrine to be sound in theory.
No longer dreary I'm alive to go and thrive and
strive for this new adventure. Be it so pure to see
clearly what I nearly did miss. Through mist and
thick haze I became amazed at what was unlocked.
What knocked me off my feet was something truly
stunning to see. Disbelief was a quick lie to try and
stop me from uncovering my true, yet wild destiny;
or at least, what I just might believe it very well is.
It's a risk nonetheless. Success begets a mess through
which only our true calling can bring us through. So
yes, it's true what they say. Utter dismay is the sign
that you are fine. To incline and certainly engage
your trust into something, that must be lost. At least
for the time being you may seem lost. Yet it cost
nothing. Changing the present for future dependents
thinking relies on the sinking together of two abstract
objects; your talent and your mind. For once they
are intertwined in such a way, no outside force will

have say to what happens next. In essence, you will control the outcome. Life will go from drudgery to actually being fun because you have become one with yourself. Not wealth but great health will come to you during this time. Don't be a mime to the adventures life has placed in front of you. Just stir the stew and see what will suddenly appear. You'll be endeared and enthralled by it all. Don't fall for the sayings of people who are raging with pessimism. Make a decision to cut them out. Only your beliefs and true doubts matter. The splatter of their words cause a curve to your learning. You're burning bright for so much more. What's in store for you will blow you away. So on this day simply stop and make a promise to be honest by letting your talents run gallantly where they please. With this ease in mind it would show how kind the Universe really is. I can tell you one thing; I know you will be blessed, because I, simply, can see success.

Did You See It Too?

Did you see it too? The circular motion of a true
devotion swirling in creativity? I give pity to the eyes
which are wrapped in lies, covered from seeing such
a sight. Might I so incline you to take a picture of this
divine intertwining, event taking place? Don't worry,
keep your pace; it's not going anywhere unless you
scare it away. Utter dismay of the highest phase has
grasped me. Clearly, this is a sign from yours to mine;
our vision does seem to mind this. The abyss of true
beauty never seemed to be rooting up and out of the
scene in such a special moment. No one could see
it, or should I say this, for the simple pleasure of it
all gives no measure of withdrawal from the ground.
Seriously, do you see it too? How shrewd the voice
to which caused this noise, making it appear. No beer
or thick liquor could bring such a quicker, or more
quickly plea for the vision in which I see. Is it real?
I only ask because I cannot feel it but this does seem
to fit my mood. Not construed but in touch with such
a noble understanding of what has happened. No
caption could describe what lies in front of my eyes.
A surprise from a lost friend couldn't even then draw
me away from this voracious witnessing of such a
happily fulfilling sight of recompense. Please, do not
get tense. Simply relax because the fact is this; if we
dismiss this event by making any sort of movement,
it will cause me to be utterly distraught. For just

this sighting has given me so much knowledge.
Even through my infinite days in college I had not
absorbed such an orb of information. The sensation is
a vibration amongst its own state. Can you also relate
to what I'm saying? Or am I naming an unjust feeling
which no such healing could cure? So pure is it right
now. How can this be? Then suddenly it disappeared.
Never have I been so near to such a vexatious beauty
of a thing. It did bring me true joy. It employed me
to see perfection without the neglection of life. But I
never did get a response to my nuance of questions.
Did you see it too?

The Future is Looking Bright

The future is looking bright. Don't get me wrong,
there's a song that says violence will never stop.
But, the future is still looking bright. Through dim
skies and slender eyes, intelligence is being passed
on. Never gone but pawned right before the dawn,
to the next generation. There's no separation in this
as a fact. You don't pass on teaching the next person
reaching to help mankind. It'd be fine if we all knew
this, but most don't. Either that or they won't admit
to it being the perfect fit for why wisdom is passed
down. No need to frown at this though; for it shows
all of us as being brighter than a lighter, or light,
to guide each race. This race at which our pace is
starting to get better. Following the steps to the letter
we are steadily making progress. We are beginning
to share, or at least getting there, when it comes to
dividing up the greed in which we have. Not that our
path is indeed used for math that's in need for all of
us to have success. But it's the finish at the end that
truly matters. And you know what? Finally, we are
starting to see who our enemies are in this race; our
emotions. While greed makes its plea we see our
happiness, in itself, in the lead. Where sadness is on
its way, we pray one day it will give up; just so we
can cup victory in our hands. But yes, the future is
certainly looking bright. Giving flight to the sight of
new technology that simply will deplete our need for

in volatile information. We feel the sensation of the nation to the point where we can easily recognize and define what it means. Although, it truly may seem keen to note one thing. That thing being this; what we know and what we bring are entirely different. Our knowledge appears from our college careers as being very helpful. So despite all the fright caused from self-doubt and lost might, the future remains still, looking bright.

Changing Seasons

Its funny how life changes. One day in May you're
enjoying the weather. Never thinking but slowly
sinking into the season of winter. It does render us
into colder temperatures. But it would be wrong
to say we can't enjoy the cold too. Through snow
fights and small plights of sledding, we all find a
way to make things better. That is a mentality built
in us all. It enthralls us to seek even the meekest
amounts of positivity. Through creativity we find a
sign of hope. It really is a beautiful thing. It's our
nature to stay firm, even in the tightest of situations.
It's the negation of a fact to react to what happens
around us. We must find a trust that all problems
are odd; but yet, they are always solvable. Some
are dissolvable while others may take a little work.
The perk of this though, is that we grow and learn
from the many mistakes we make. It takes some
persistence and the resistance is eminent, but it does
lament in due time. It's kind of like a marathon
runner. Though it's funner, or more fun, when the
run isn't for competition. The attention given during
a regular race is a fight. Not of might, but of will.
Until you realize that being fast does not last, you
will always lose. You must choose to simply focus
on finishing. No diminishing results will come if you
know this. True bliss is sought out when the doubts
in pessimistic thought are left alone. To own your

thoughts is to live a great life. It's a rudimentary idea but to see what the end results bring makes it completely worth it. Nevertheless, success is the best way to stay blessed. It gives an interest to the many changing seasons.

The Systematic Plot

A mystic demise, with a sustainable surprise.

How often have we fallen, to a number of these lies.

No wonder why we're lost, there has been no real
truth.

Yet greatness is your search, nothing short of its
reproof.

Let's take a second and think, what is it that we
remember?

Among the constellations, few stars are shown
forever.

So what's that say for us, we can't all shine that
bright?

Or maybe there's a way, to be seen throughout the
night?

We don't need a poetic genius, nor a country famous
star.

Not a rapper with remorse, nor a person above
subpar.

We need sight for brighter lights, a creative future plan.

One that brings out the potential, without the eerie found demands.

A person who is focused, is the personified belief.

And a person who is wayward, only sees their newest grief.

So our society is off, that's okay we'll get right back.

For trains were built despite the fact, there were no laid out tracks.

So simply it is mentally, a challenge worth an answer.

So maybe in a shorter time, we'll rid this newest cancer.

But till then take some time alone, to stay in deeper thought.

Only then we'll end what now begins, the systematic plot.

Foresight

Taking all the time I have and writing down my
  thoughts.

I've come to match some new findings and realized
  there's a lot.

A lot of this and some of that mixed with some "that's
  insane!"

It got my juices flowing, well, enough to pick my
  brain.

"Could this be right?" I said aloud and "Is this really
  true?"

How is it that no one's seen this, these facts must be
  construed.

I read it twice and then five times to make sure that
  it's right.

"It seems correct" I say out loud, it flows just like a
  kite.

I shared these thoughts with all my friends and they
  seemed so appalled.

They knew not how these thoughts were true, but
    knew what to recall.

So on and on they went their way to tell of this old
    news.

I say it's old because it's plain and came from all past
    views.

So history is just the past that shows us what's to
    come.

But maybe it's the past that shows foresight on where
    we're from.

And if we know where we are from we'll know then
    where to go.

This is the simple logic that I've read and come to
    know.

Now who's to prove these writings wrong when
    clearly they are used?

Not once or twice but every day by those who buy the
    news.

And those who don't still know that their own past
    helps them to learn.

All things may change or stay the same no matter
what we earn.

So know one thing if you do choose to use this for
your life.

Keep just the past in the last seat and learn to lose the
strife.

For looking back can cause a crash for any future fun.

So let foresight keep your eyes straight and finish
what's undone.

A Desperate Eye

A desperate eye sees very little. The blinding stages
for those who major in bottom feeding are all too
common. They look for those who also chose to be
despicable things. Thieves and dealers, Drug Lords
and killers are amongst the few. Who's to say they
can't be stopped? They take and learn the mistakes
that earned them this type of living. But, its not
necessarily their fault. They came from families that
only wished to see their own greed's fulfilled. They
never had a chance. But the stance to wear the pants
of the upright can still be chosen. They might be
comfortable but notice they stumble on more than
one occasion. I'm sure they'll come to make the right
choice. Not for the gain but to replace the pain their
past has dealt them. They've been in the street, trying
to retreat from the defeat; yet, they are trapped. Not
in a prison but a prism of their own mindset. Thank
God you are not there with them. The only way out
is to doubt everything they once learned. Imagine
two plus two no longer equaling four. Never before
has one ignored such adoration in a sound doctrine of
thought. That is what they face. Disgrace everyday
makes them hide from a race they never prepared for.
It's not right though to tell them they are wrong. Give
them some options not forgotten, or forgetting, that
you yourself were once confused at how life worked.
Show them a life where strife doesn't knife them in

the back. They need to see that. But look at us giving them advice. We need to learn to earn their yearning attitude for a better life. They worked through the danger to anger their haters. They are demonstrators of taking what they believe is theirs. It's only fair to share this knowledge. You don't need a degree to see, that a desperate eye sees very little.

Only Time Will Tell

Only time will tell. It's not a spell in which a remedy
can fix; but time will tell. It could tell us to crawl
from defeat or to go and retrieve what's been long
missing. Fixing what's been broken for years takes
tears and hard work, but time has the last say. Each
day we manifest a new test to put ourselves through.
We prove we can last the doubts of past stimulations
through the deprivation of its present directs. For
respect we lay wait, the hate, for our neighbors. We
endure this for one reason; time is in control. Not
to hold us back but to attract our attention to future
visions we wish to see through. No clue as to which
switch will turn this dream to what's real, we feel
around for a sense as to what tense in time this will
happen. We tap in to ourselves for inner stealth
for a better look. What shook you at that moment
wasn't imaginary but on the contrary a small fairy
of an ounce of magic. Tragic how dramatic our
subconscious can be when we still try to intercede it
for help. No wealth comes from it but the sense of
being at peace takes the least of our domains. Simple
names come to mind of who truly is inclined for our
happiness. Never to sense that we are the ones who
are in control of this factor. "The reactor," you may
ask, is the task we haven't yet claimed to see; yet,
don't fret on this. Bliss is on its way to say that on this
day, only time will tell.

Another Element

Another element was found. What's going on is
something long from what we know. We sow ideas of
being fields ahead; when really, we're dealing with
something unknown. King to its own throne we've
blown our cover in the operation. Through situational
status, we've had it for far too long of a time. Let
me ease your mind with this; what is unknown isn't
necessarily a danger. A stranger yes, but through it
progress can be made. Never raid it for intelligence
but use common sense to learn. Earn its trust so
lust does not deceive your own thoughts. It can't
be bought or taught; simply observed. It deserves
that much respect since our dialect computes only
amongst ourselves. With a wealth of information
remember each sensation it gives off. Aloft the mist
it will fix what you thought to be broken, dry those
that are soaking, and give words to those who have
not spoken up; but good luck to those without this
truth. A roof holds in the thoughts within your own
cube. It's only when someone intrudes your box that
great things are unlocked to your present problem. To
solve them you must've known this scent; that there is
indeed, another element.

The Promise

Do you remember the promise? It was made years ago
by the thorough souls of this Earth. Giving birth to new
minds they felt inclined to give their words; a promise.
Though let's be honest, does anybody remember
what it was? The buzz of this news was not true until
one day. They decided to say what the promise was.
With this being said the heads of many turned to hear
what this promise meant. It was God-sent to anoint
those who did point toward success. Every chest was
filled with a guild of empowerment and joy. Though
annoyed, they were still curious about it. A bit was
said but nothing gave troubling happiness after it was
announced. No one pounced at the ideas of which they
spoke. There was one line that stayed in mind though.
"Keep free from greed and intercede all problems
with God for him to solve them; for we cannot." Well
wasn't this a weird plot. No one knew what this shrewd
saying did mean, so clean was their conscious at the
time. Only mimes to the cause, they went along with
what they were doing. Till the moving of their lives
took place. Disaster and disgrace remained to claim
lives and many died, not knowing what to say or do.
Yet one of the few remembered the promise. He lived
to give this knowledge to all who would listen though
the resisters did perish. He told people to be honest and
astonish on nothing else, and then he asked, "Do you
remember the promise?"

Fitting Times

Times change to your fitting. Your perspective gives an elective outlook on life. You choose what you lose, though what's lost may be confused with what you never needed. Preceded are the thoughts of a lot more, though at the time what you needed to see bored your very being. Interesting isn't it? Time really does change to your fitting. Whether it's gritting your teeth through a struggle, or troubled thoughts may keep you locked in a poisonous mindset; yet, your life shows no regret or remorse. You could be poor and old but happily bold in everything you do, bringing you great satisfaction. Or in reaction, you could be young and rich but twitch at the very thought of everything being alright. It's a fight to keep the right outlook on life. Only lies deny this. Negative thoughts come but what's won in this battle is up to you. Positivity is an activity you must practice. You get better with time so when signs of trouble head your way your mindset can be at bay with what currently takes place. You can face your fears. Wow, just to hear that brings back what lack we do have in our optimism. See it's a prism in our conscious that makes us nauseous when we think about it in the wrong way. Who's to say anything is not possible? The throes in life can be hard but barge through it. You can see fit that the legit results will come to you. The truth in this matter does scatter the platter from which we must eat from. Being one does not run us out of our own proclivity. It simply shows our ability to act. So with this fact in life's bidding, you must know; that time, does change to our fitting.

Simple Plans

His plan for you is simple. He's seen you at your
lowest but know it's not the hindrance for your
success. He says its something else. What's felt isn't
always right but the plight to your overcoming starts
with realigning what you know. You grow with the
knots that untie when your thoughts align with his.
He's seen when you were dismissed. When the fists
of hurtful words did blur your vision for yourself. You
thought people were correct in their select demeaning
usage of your kindness. Though their blindness was
spoken in their needs for good jokes when simply,
they wanted something you have. Maybe it's the
path, or better yet the map, to living a fulfilling life.
Their strife bares too much for them to wish you
luck on their own. But what's known is this. His
promise will not change. It may seem strange how
it works but the murky water will clear soon. The
moon can be seen during days where it seems sunny.
So what makes you think you can't prove the world
wrong? That's his true mission, bringing haters to
submission under your right doings. He's suing the
court so you can report to your rightful duties. The
ruby is brighter when you're flying higher than the
rest. So dismiss these full grown pests, because the
test for your success will be coming shortly. He's here
so you don't do poorly on it. He won't give you the
answers because your mind is the planter for the most

intelligent seed. His need is simply to remind you of that. The fact is that, you can do it. You'll make it through it and prove it is possible to accomplish even the most impossible feats. Don't retreat but move forward so those moving toward the light can meet you there. Be fair in your judgment and know that you were sent by Him. Just know you can stand because he truly does, have simple plans.

Insight: Tomorrow

We'll never know why we're dealt the hand we have in life. We'll never know why we struggle where others succeed. We'll never know why some prayers go unanswered. There are a lot of things we'll never know or understand about life. But I do know one thing. Tomorrow is a chance for better days. Tomorrow is a chance for you to break your addiction. Tomorrow is a chance for you to overcome your fears. Tomorrow is a chance to get the girl or guy of your dreams. And you know what, tomorrow is the only thing we need. If we can make it through the night and reach tomorrow, we can do anything. We can change the nation. We can break a generational curse. We can do anything we want with tomorrow. Sadly, some people don't make it to tomorrow. So instead of feeling guilty, realize that tomorrow your slate is wiped clean. Tomorrow, well . . . . tomorrow is hope. Hope for a better life than your living today. So don't worry about your problems. Don't worry about your shortcomings. You just focus on tomorrow. Tomorrow isn't promised to anyone, but if you make it to tomorrow, you can make it through anything. Tomorrow is the only thing that matters.

Acknowledgements

This was a very hard book to write. It's never easy to put down personal experiences and thoughts on paper for the whole world to see. Yet, it was very rewarding at the same time. Thankfully I had a lot of encouragement from friends and family to help me to write this.

I would like to thank both of my parents, Robert and Winnie Warren, for bearing with me on this project. They could have easily told me it was a waste of time. Instead, they encouraged me to continue writing and to eventually put this book into publication. I would like to thank my brother and best friend, Eric Warren, who not only read every last poem, but also encouraged others to read it too. I would like to thank my good friend, Toyosi Azeez, who was one of the first to encourage me to do this project. I thank God for affording me this opportunity to use what I have in order to help and inspire others.

There is a great many other people I would like to thank: AuthorHouse Publishing, my Publishing Consultant Terry Johnson, Lyle Philips, and the great editors at AuthorHouse. With that being said, I would like to thank everyone who encouraged me to do this project and complimented some of the poems that I put in this book. To those who have chosen to read this book, I would like to thank you too. I hope you enjoyed it and encourage you to share it with others if it helped you in any way. Be blessed and stay blessed.

About The Author

Alex K. Warren was born in Dallas, Texas. He and his family ended up moving to a small factory city—Lima, Ohio—when he was just two years old. It was a city with many abandoned buildings, and even less hope. However, he learned to trust and believe in a better future for his self through his upbringings in a Christian home. He graduated from The Ohio State University with a Bachelor's degree in Broadcasting and Communications within three years. He has been published twice in the Lantern Newspaper (Ohio State's newspaper) and has had the privilege of working alongside the Big Ten Network. He goes around the city of Lima, and other small cities, to relay the message that there is hope and a whole world out there that is waiting for their young minds to discover; despite their upbringings and situations. As he has said, "A successful future is always achievable, it simply takes some belief."